# THE CREATIVE USE OF MUSIC
# IN GROUP THERAPY

## ABOUT THE AUTHOR

Tom Plach is a 1975 graduate of The DePaul School of Music in Chicago, Illinois. He practiced as a music therapist for eight years before receiving his master's degree in social work from The Jane Addams College of Social Work at The University of Illinois at Chicago. Tom is a licensed clinical social worker in Illinois, as well as being a registered music therapist. His other publication is *Residential Treatment and the Sexually Abused Child,* published by Charles C Thomas in 1993.

## Second Edition

# THE CREATIVE USE OF MUSIC IN GROUP THERAPY

*By*

TOM PLACH, R.M.T., L.C.S.W.

CHARLES C THOMAS • PUBLISHER
*Springfield • Illinois • U.S.A.*

*Published and Distributed Throughout the World by*

**CHARLES C THOMAS • PUBLISHER**
2600 South First Street
Springfield, Illinois 62794-9265

© *1996 by* CHARLES C THOMAS • PUBLISHER

ISBN 0-398-06585-3 (cloth)
ISBN 0-398-06586-1 (paper)

Library of Congress Catalog Card Number: 95-50966

First Edition, 1980

Second Edition, 1996

*With* THOMAS BOOKS *careful attention is given to all details of manufacturing
and design. It is the Publisher's desire to present books that are satisfactory as to
their physical qualities and artistic possibilities and appropriate for their particular
use.* THOMAS BOOKS *will be true to those laws of quality that assure a good
name and good will.*

*Printed in the United States of America*
*SC-R-3*

**Library of Congress Cataloging-in-Publication Data**

Plach, Tom.
    The creative use of music in group therapy / by Tom Plach. — 2nd
ed.
        p.      cm.
    Includes bibliographical references and index.
    ISBN 0-398-06585-3 (cloth). — ISBN 0-398-06586-1 (pbk.)
    1. Group psychotherapy.   2. Music therapy.   3. Group psychotherapy
for teenagers.   I. Title.
RC488.P59      1996
816.89'1654—dc20                                                                    95-50966
                                                                                          CIP

*To Thaina*

# PREFACE

I n the past forty years, the use of music and music activities as a form of therapy has become increasingly popular and more accepted by professionals in all aspects of the helping professions. Music therapy is currently being employed in all aspects of psychiatric care, homes for the retarded, and homes for the aged. It is also being used with the physically handicapped, developmentally disabled, sensory impaired, and in special education within the school systems. Universities and colleges everywhere are developing and implementing degree programs in music therapy, both at the undergraduate and the graduate level, so as to meet the increasing demand for qualified music therapists. Despite the rapid growth of the field, however, there seems to be a lack of published material on how to use music as a form of therapy. A brief overview of currently available resources in music therapy shows an abundance of excellent research material,[1] a minimal amount of published books on music therapy with the retarded, music therapy with special education, music therapy with the aged, and music activities for psychiatric clients. There are also several excellent books that give overviews of the field of music therapy. Taking into account this severe shortage of available materials on music therapy, the purpose of this book is to offer the reader information on one small aspect of the overall field of music therapy; this being the use of music in conjunction with group therapy for the adolescent and adult psychiatric client.

The book is designed for the student who is just beginning a career in human services as well as for the experienced professional seeking to add new techniques to their repertoire of treatment approaches. While the guidelines and examples presented in the book highlight the needs of the client in an inpatient psychiatric setting, the formats are adaptable

---

[1]For a concise overview of the research that is available in music therapy, I would refer the reader to the *Music Therapy Index*, available through the National Association for Music Therapy, P. O. Box 610, Lawrence, Kansas 66044.

to other settings as well. This can include the outpatient mental health setting, the residential treatment setting, the inpatient medical unit, the substance abuse treatment program, or intermediate care facility. For, regardless of the setting or the presenting problem of the client, music can be easily blended into a group therapy program.

*The Creative Use of Music in Group Therapy,* therefore, is an attempt to help the professional human services worker develop an added skill to benefit the client. It is with this foundation that I present *The Creative Use of Music in Group Therapy.*

# ACKNOWLEDGMENTS

Special thanks to Twentieth Century Music Corporation, Fox Fanfare Music, Inc., for the use of lyrics to "Home" by Charlie Smalls, copyright © 1974, 1975, and 1978 by Fox Fanfare Music, Inc.; all rights reserved. Used by permission.

# CONTENTS

*When we feel, we begin to be alive. When we express a feeling, we share with the rest of the world that we are alive. When we express a feeling through music, we invite the rest of the world to share in our experience of the feeling, and to be alive with us.*

# THE CREATIVE USE OF MUSIC
# IN GROUP THERAPY

# Chapter I

# INTRODUCTION

"I think she should get out of the situation altogether."
"No. She would be better off if she stayed where she was at."
"But she's not happy there."
"But it's secure. Why change something that is safe and secure."

The preceding dialogue was being held by several clients in a group therapy session that was begun with music. The basis of the discussion was the lyrics in a popular song entitled "Lyin' Eyes,"[2] to which the group had listened at the start of the session. The song describes a young woman who is involved in a romantic triangle, which has apparently left her feeling unhappy and unfulfilled. The song also points out the woman's tendency to maintain the behavioral pattern that led to her present situation. The clients in the group session were in the process of exploring this behavioral pattern, the benefits involved in maintaining the pattern, and some possible solutions to the problem. Later on in the session, the clients began to apply the same problem-solving process to their own personal issues, thus gaining some new insights about how they create problems in their own lives. The clients also discovered that, as individual members of a group, they all had something in common, i.e. patterns of behavior that resulted in their feeling unfulfilled. What made this session unique was that many of the clients had previously been resistive to or defensive toward the leader's attempts to facilitate personal insights. Because the clients had seen the problem somewhere else first, i.e. through a character in a song, they seemed able to let down their defenses and, as a result, explore something new to them.

This example is one of many techniques for applying music in a group therapy session. Definitively, music therapy can be described as the use of music in the accomplishment of therapeutic aims. Specifically, music as it applies to group therapy can be defined as the use of music or music activities as a stimulus for promoting new behaviors in and explor-

---

[2]"Lyin' Eyes," recorded by the Eagles on Asylum Records.

3

ing predetermined individual or group goals in a group setting. This book shall explore two different formats for a group therapy session with music. The first format, which will be exclusively addressed in Chapter III, involves using music or a music activity at the start of the session, allowing the remainder of the session for processing group and individual reactions to the activity. This particular format tends to focus on the stages involved in personal growth and group development as well as encouraging exploration of and personal work on pertinent therapeutic issues.

The second format, which will be addressed in Chapter V, involves the use of a music activity throughout an entire group therapy session. This format does not set aside specific time for the participants to process reactions to the activity. Within this format, the major focus is usually upon the acquisition of recreational and interpersonal skills as well as upon the fun aspect of music.

Before moving into these areas, however, it seems necessary to explore some of the advantages of using music in group therapy. To do this, let us take a statement from a client involved in group therapy with music, for who would know better the advantages of having music in a session than an inpatient who attends five or six nonmusic group therapy sessions a week. Said one middle-aged female client, "Music helps me feel. I experience things in this group that I never experience in other groups." The same client went on to elaborate upon how music frequently puts her in touch with sadness that she often avoids confronting as well as with other feelings she attempts to block out. Juliette Alvin, in her book entitled *Music Therapy,* elaborates even further on this particular advantage:

> Even in its most simple forms, music is evocative of sensations, moods, and emotions. It can reflect the feeling of the moment or change it by its presence. It can also increase the actual mood and bring it to a climax or dispel it.[3]

She later continues,

> Music has the power to affect mood because it contains suggestive, persuasive, or even compelling elements. In music accompanying a specific function one of these elements is usually dominant. But whatever its purpose music is always related to man's own experiences, since it has been born out of his mind, speaks of his emotions, and lies within his perceptual range.[4]

---

[3]Juliette Alvin, *Music Therapy* (New York, Basic Books, Inc., 1975), p. 60.
[4]*Ibid.,* p. 61.

The therapist who has facilitated group therapy with no stimulus but his own dialogue and body language can certainly identify with the difficulty involved in bringing to the surface feelings or issues that the participants constantly avoid. Yet, music seems to be able to sneak in the back way. Where direct dialogue or confrontation may have met with extreme defensiveness and anxiety, music may open up communication between therapist and client.

The best example of music as a resource for evoking feelings, however, is our own individual experiences with music. I would invite the reader to spend a few minutes contemplating the following questions: What music do you like to listen to when you are sad? Angry? Happy? When was the last time a song brought a tear to your eye? What five songs do you most identify with and why? What songs do you most dislike? If you were to write a song, what would it be about? What musical instrument would best describe how you feel right now?

Given that most people could answer the above questions, we once again see a potentially valuable resource for evoking feelings, as well as expression of thoughts and feelings. What evokes feelings in each of us as individual human beings, and what provides each of us individually with a vehicle for expression, certainly has the potential for a similar impact upon a group.

To further elaborate upon this technique of using music as a vehicle for self-expression, let us look at the various degrees of complication that could potentially be involved in expressing oneself through music. A highly complicated form of self-expression through music, for example, might be a 100-person choral group performing a difficult vocal selection. Although each member of the chorus may be singing something slightly different from the other members, the result is an individual and group expression of a particular feeling and/or idea. Within the framework of a group therapy session, self-expression through music might take a much simpler form. For example, a session might be composed of each client expressing a feeling on a selected rhythm instrument, first individually and then collectively as a part of the group. Self-expression through music might also take the form of each client selecting a song that is expressive of something that he feels and then singing that song alone or with the group. In whatever form it takes, music can provide a valuable and effective alternative for self-expression for the client who has difficulty expressing himself through verbal dialogue or nonverbal movements.

Besides being able to evoke specific feelings and thoughts in the individual and group, and besides being a vehicle for self-expression, music is also very adept at stimulating verbalizations and socialization. The most common example of this power is the quiet, shy individual who attends a group sing-along, hears some of his favorite songs, and suddenly is singing and socializing with the group. As was pointed out earlier, music is related to man's own experience and is a vehicle of expression for his thoughts and feelings. What one man is able to express through music, other men can relate to inwardly on an emotional level and outwardly on a verbal level.

The final major advantage for employing music in a group therapy session lies in its reliability in offering a group a common and dependable starting place for discussion and personal work. As with any other stimulative technique, the group leader using music has no guarantee that his group will respond in a certain manner on a given day to a preselected music activity. However, because of its ability to evoke similar emotions, thoughts, and behavioral responses within various listeners,[5] the leader can often predict with some certainty how his group will respond to a given musical activity. This, then, provides the leader with a valuable tool for facilitating responses. An experienced and knowledgeable music therapist can conceivably take any group of clients, at any level of functioning, at any given point in time, and with minimal knowledge of the individual illnesses and group dynamics, design and implement a music activity that will facilitate exploration and growth on an important issue for the group or its individual members. As will be stressed throughout this book, even when the group does not respond in the manner expected by the leader, a good facilitator can turn the experience into a therapeutic learning experience for the participants.

Throughout the remainder of this book, many of the other advantages

---

[5]The assumption that music has the ability to evoke similar emotions and behavioral responses in people comes from two basic sources. The first is my own personal observations and experiences with facilitating hundreds of groups of clients. In using much of the same music repeatedly, I have been able to observe similar emotional and verbal reactions in different groups listening to the same music. This leads me to believe that many of us will react in similar ways to a given musical selection, although our reactions can be altered at any time by such factors as personal mood, present environmental circumstances, etc. The second source on which this assumption is based is the wealth of research that has been done in measuring people's responses to a given selection of music. Although the research is varied, the majority of research in this area seems to attempt to measure people's likes/dislikes for and/or their emotional reactions to music and then correlate those measurements with such factors as age, sex, or personality traits. Although much of the research tends to substantiate the claim that music can evoke similar emotions and thoughts in people, I would invite the interested reader to explore the research personally through the *Music Therapy Index* mentioned in footnote 1.

of using music in group therapy will be shown via concrete examples of activities. The four advantages pointed out thus far regarding ability to evoke feelings, ability to provide a vehicle for expression, ability to stimulate verbalizations, and reliability to provide a common starting place are major advantages and, thus, have received special attention.

## PERSPECTIVES

Over the past seventy-five to 100 years, numerous models of group therapy and group therapy techniques have been developed and proven to be effective. To view group music therapy in its proper perspective, it might be advantageous to explore how it fits into or is similar to preexisting models.

Upon initial observance, group therapy through music seems closely related to the Theme Centered Interactional Method developed by Ruth Cohn.[6] As in this particular model, group music therapy sessions are often built around a preselected theme or issue that the group desires or is required to explore. For instance, in the example given at the start of the chapter in which the group members were discussing the lyrics to the song "Lyin' Eyes," the preselected theme was how people set themselves up to feel unfulfilled. Hence, a song was selected that might help the group explore that theme. Unlike the Theme Centered Interactional Method, however, in group music therapy the theme is rarely ever stated at the start of the session. By stating a specific theme at the beginning of a music session, the leader immediately sets up an expectation of how the clients should respond to the music. Since listening to music is considered a subjective experience, with no right way or wrong way to experience it, the communication of such an expectation will only lead to internal conflict within the listener, i.e. "do I respond in the way the leader expects me to respond, or how I really am responding?" This particular issue of possibly influencing client responses is addressed at greater length in Chapter II, "Guidelines for a Music Therapy Session."

A group therapy session in music may also differ from the Theme Centered Interactional Method in respect to the amount of emphasis placed, by the leader, upon remaining focused on the original preselected theme. The leader in a group music therapy session, for example, may

---

[6]Ruth Cohn, "Theme Centered Model," in John B.P. Shaffer and M. David Galinsky, *Group Therapy and Sensitivity Training* (Englewood Cliffs, Prentice-Hall, 1974), pp. 242–264.

not emphasize focusing on the original theme, particularly when there is a large degree of variation between the group's initial response to the activity and the preselected theme. In referring once again to our example of the group discussing "Lyin' Eyes," it is conceivable that after listening to the song, several clients may begin crying or showing other signs of being emotionally upset. In such a case, instead of putting pressure on the group to problem solve for the character in the song as might have been originally planned, the leader will shift the focus to having the emotionally upset client(s) work on interacting with the group about his feelings. In other words, the leader will choose to facilitate the responses to the music activity that occur with the group regardless of the relation of the responses to the preselected theme.

When selecting the theme or issue for a group music therapy session, the leader will, in some respects, employ concepts from the various group dynamic models of group therapy. A basic concept involved in the group dynamic model is that all group therapy sessions can be characterized in terms of a single overriding focus or concern, i.e. focal conflict. In the Foulke[7] model of group dynamics, this might refer to a theme or common concern within the group. Henry Ezriel,[8] in his model, refers to this theme as the "common group tension," whereas Dorothy Stock Whitaker and Morten A. Lieberman[9] refer to this as a conflict between a disturbing motive and a reactive motive. Part of the job confronting the therapist, who must preplan a music activity for a group, is to identify its common theme or focal conflict and then select an activity that would help facilitate group and individual focus upon the theme.

For example, let us say that over a period of several sessions the leader observes several clients initiating the topic of anger within the group. However, each time the topic surfaces, the subject gets changed very rapidly. The leader might observe the clients becoming increasingly anxious and more defensive each time the topic of anger arises. Several clients might also be observed behaving in ways that the leader could

---

[7]Foulkes approach to group dynamics, as presented in John B.P. Shaffer and M. David Galinsky, *Group Therapy and Sensitivity Training* (Englewood Cliffs, Prentice-Hall, 1974), pp. 73–76.

[8]Henry Ezriel, approach to group dynamics, as presented in John B.P. Shaffer and M. David Galinsky, *Group Therapy and Sensitivity Training* (Englewood Cliffs, Prentice-Hall, 1974), pp. 76–78.

[9]Dorothy Stock Whitaker, Morton A. Lieberman approach to group dynamics, as presented in John B.P. Shaffer and M. David Galinsky, *Group Therapy and Sensitivity Training* (Englewood Cliffs, Prentice-Hall, 1974), pp. 78–80.

interpret as indirect expressions of anger toward each other. Given these observations, anger could then be looked upon as possibly being a common group tension or a common concern within the group. The leader might then choose to structure a music activity that would help the clients focus upon the topic of anger while simultaneously lowering the clients' defensiveness.

Within the course of a number of sessions, a creative therapist can also integrate techniques or concepts from various other models of group therapy into a group music therapy session. Some of these other models might include psychodrama (incorporation of background mood music into the drama process), behavior therapy (music used as a reinforcement for behavior), group psychoanalytic model (interpretation or analysis of clients' fantasy trips done to music), and various models of group encounter. Generally, it is up to the leader to decide which models best lend themselves to the groups' needs as well as to his own personal style of facilitation.

Thus, although group therapy through music may be closely related to several particular models of group therapy, it may also be integrated into other models as well. In terms of its applicability to various groups of clientele, group music therapy can be adapted to fit a variety of needs. It can be employed within the institutional setting with long-term, chronically mentally client as well as the client experiencing an acute mental health problem. Also within the institutional setting, group music therapy may be integrated into a team approach program, into milieu therapy, or it may be used strictly on a referral basis. Group music therapy can also be employed with the sensory impaired or physically disabled client, whether in or out of the institutional setting. Various programs of outpatient treatment may integrate group music therapy, as might the professional in private practice. Music can be incorporated into group therapy sessions on a daily or weekly basis, or it might be used as an occasional aid in the overall process of the group. Wherever, whenever, whoever, or however music is integrated into group therapy, it can be a valuable asset in helping the group and its members meet its goals.

Having given this brief overview on group therapy through music, let us move on to explore some basic guidelines for planning, implementing, and facilitating a group music therapy session.

# Chapter II

# GUIDELINES FOR GROUP
# MUSIC THERAPY SESSIONS

When I think of home,
I think of a place where there's
Love overflowing;
I wish I was home,
I wish I was back there,
With the things I've been knowing.*

In using music in the group therapy setting, there are eight basic guidelines for the leader to follow. The first three guidelines address the issue of selecting an appropriate activity for the group. This issue is of utmost importance, since selecting the wrong activity at the wrong time for the wrong group of clients could potentially lead to an uncomfortable situation for the leader as well as a nontherapeutic experience for the clients.

The next guideline addresses the role of the leader as it pertains to the music activity. This is not to be confused with the issue of what the overall role of a leader is in group therapy. This particular issue has been addressed numerous times in many books about group therapy. Although the overall role of a leader in group therapy is an important consideration in group music therapy, it is also a consideration that must be done individually, according to one's own beliefs. Therefore, this book will will focus upon the role of the leader only as it pertains to the music activity.

The final four guidelines suggest various methods of using the music activity to help facilitate the session. These four guidelines, of course, do not presume to cover the entire realm of possibilities for processing and facilitating a group session. They do, however, give the beginning therapist some concrete ideas for using the music activity to help facilitate the group, once the session has begun.

---

The eight guidelines for planning and implementing music in group therapy are as follows:

1. The chosen activity should be appropriately in tune with individual symptomatology, individual and group needs, and within whatever conceptual, integrative, or physical limitations are existent within the group.
2. Music chosen for a session must take into consideration cultural and age factors existent within the group.
3. The amount of structure contained in the activity is contingent upon the level of functioning of the group and its individual members.
4. The level of participation by the leader in the music activity is determined by what the group needs to experience the activity to its fullest potential.
5. All individual and group responses to a music activity are valid responses.
6. Whenever appropriate, communicate immediate observations of behavior in the music activity to the group and/or individuals in the group.
7. Whenever appropriate, refer back to the initial activity and group or individual responses to the activity.
8. Whenever appropriate, explore within the group ways of integrating newfound insights, behaviors, or skills into situations outside of the group.

In referring back to the first three guidelines, one of the first tasks the leader must complete before planning an activity is to obtain a general sense of the level of functioning of his group and the individuals in it. The leader can usually gain this sense by answering questions such as, Do they initiate contact with each other, and if so, what type of contact is initiated? Are the members verbally responsive? What is their degree of reality orientation? How long is their attention span? How energetic are they, both as a group and as individuals? As a group, at what stage of development are they? By answering questions such as these, the leader begins to get a sense of what to expect from the group, what their needs are, and what limitations exist within the group. He can then plan his activity according to the first three guidelines.

According to the first guideline, the leader must be aware of some of the important dynamics in his group. The leader must use caution not to encourage or feed into unhealthy symptomatology. For example, a group in which several members are known to have hallucinations would certainly not be appropriate for a fantasy trip to music. The fantasy itself would most likely encourage or feed into the hallucinations.

The leader must also be certain that the activity chosen is within the realm of conceptualization, integrative functions, and physical limitations of the group members. A leader cannot expect a group to perform a task that its members cannot accomplish because of physical or mental limitations. For example, a leader cannot realistically expect a group where the members experience profound mental retardation to benefit from a discussion of emotional isolation if the retardation interferes with the ability to conceptualize such a concept. A more appropriate activity for such a group might be a simplified activity that encourages social contact between the members.

Also, in planning the activity, the leader needs to develop a sense of what the group needs are and what the needs of the individual members are. For example, a leader might know that the group is at a stage of development in which they are learning and exploring new insights about themselves. The leader can then take the group to a new level of development[10] by designing an activity in which the group would put the insights to use via new behavior in the group.

The leader might also know, for example, that several of the members in the group are exploring the issue of loneliness. The task would then be to choose an activity that would help the members focus on this topic, thus encouraging personal growth for those individuals.

Guideline two focuses on the importance of selecting music according to cultural tastes and age differences. To quote music psychologist Paul Farnsworth,

> Taste is lawful, however, in no absolute sense, but rather in the manner in which all social phenomena are lawful. For just as each social phenomenon is associated with a particular time and place, so is taste relative to a limited time and a narrow culture area.
>
> Indeed, to a considerable degree laymen tend to prefer and to honor whatever they think should be preferred and honored.[11]

---

[10]The term *level of development* refers to the stage of development of music therapy groups, which will be discussed in Chapter III.

[11]Paul Farnsworth, *Musical Taste—Its Measurement and Cultural Nature* (Stanford, Stanford University Press), p. 81.

The concept itself is simple. A group will not relate to or will not enjoy what it does not like, does not understand, or does not prefer or honor. A group will usually tune out or refuse to participate in music that does not correspond to its cultural background or its musical era of interest. A very blatant example of not following this guideline would be to play hard rock music for a group of senior citizens. Studies have proven that elderly adults prefer music of their young adult years[12] and, thus, would probably not participate or be interested in a session employing rock music. A leader wishing to involve a group of adolescents in a music session would probably gain more involvement and interest by using popular music as opposed to classical music.

Cultural tastes are also an important consideration when selecting music for a group therapy session. Cultural tastes as used here refers to certain interests or beliefs that are a unique part of a specific ethnic or religious group. Certain styles of music are known to be more widely accepted within specific cultures, while certain styles of music appear to cross over cultures. When selecting music to be used in a group therapy session the leader should strive to use music that is consistent with the cultural tastes of the group members.

Choosing music appropriate to different cultural and age backgrounds clearly necessitates that the leader possess a wide background in various styles of music. Yet, this particular aspect of preplanning group music activities is so vitally important to the overall success of a session that the leader must discover ways of broadening his repertoire and knowledge of various styles of music. Without the needed background, a leader might tend to subject the group to his own personal tastes in music, thus disregarding the group's interests or needs. Although choosing music for a session according to the leader's own subjective response to the music can often be a valuable resource and asset in group therapy, the group interests and needs must always be kept in the forefront during the process of selecting music for a session.

In the third guideline, the concept of structure in an activity is focused on. Structure in a music activity refers to the degree of specific goal orientation and task assignment, and the amount of external control (via rules, policies, etc.) placed on the group through the activity. To understand this concept more clearly, it might be helpful to take one

---

[12]Alicia Clair Gibbons, "Popular Music Preferences of Elderly People," *Journal of Music Therapy,* Winter, 1977.

specific activity and explore two different methods that could conceivably be used in applying it in a session.

The potential goals set forth for the session include developing a sense of cohesiveness within the group (via accomplishment of a group assignment), and encouraging creative thinking. The activity to be used is called Musical Storytelling. In the activity the group is asked to create a story inspired by a musical selection played for them. The activity done with an extreme amount of structure might involve a process such as this: (1) The group listens to the first musical selection; (2) The therapist explains the task assignment, then begins the story himself by creating two sentences; (3) The person to the left of the leader adds two more sentences, the person to his left adds two more sentences, and so on, until the task comes back to the leader; (4) A second selection of music is played, and the story continues by repeating steps two and three; (5) A third selection of music is played, and the story is concluded by again repeating steps two and three.

The preceding example, of course, is very rigid with very little opportunity for variation from the assigned task. It does, however, provide much external control in the process, which might be helpful to a group that experiences difficulty with remaining focused on a theme or task.

The same activity done with less structure might have a process such as this: (1) The group listens to the first selection of music; (2) Group members discuss feelings or ideas inspired by the music; (3) The group leader explains the task assignment to the group and asks for a volunteer to begin the story; (4) Anyone who wishes then adds an unspecified amount of sentences to the story, until each person has contributed something; (5) A second selection of music is played, and the leader asks for a volunteer to continue the story based on the new music, (6) Step four is repeated; (7) A third selection of music is played, and the group decides as a whole how to end the story based on the final selection of music.

As might be observed, this second example offers fewer rules and limitations for the group to follow and, thus, leaves more space for variation from the activity. Rather than placing a judgment on which method is better or more therapeutic, it is important to realize that both methods can be valid, depending upon the specific group of clients. As guideline two implies, the amount of structure inherent in the activity will be contingent upon the level of functioning of the group and its members. A lower functioning group, i.e. short attention span, frequent loose associations, poor reality orientation, low level of verbal responsiveness, beginning stages of group development, etc., will ordinarily require more structure and outer control than a higher functioning group. The higher functioning group, i.e. long attention span, high level of verbal responsiveness, good contact with reality, etc., can ordinarily integrate and apply basic concepts quickly, needing less structure and outer control, and, hence, could benefit from the second process. Knowing how much structure to give a group, and knowing when the structure is stifling the group rather than facilitating it, are like a sixth sense that the leader must develop. Too much structure in an activity or in the form of leadership all too often can hinder a group's creativity and growth, whereas too little structure might leave a group without direction or purpose.

Once the activity has been selected, the next step involved is for the leader to decide what his level of participation should be in the activity. As guideline four points out, the leader's level of participation in the activity should be based on the group's needs and what he, as leader, anticipates will best help facilitate the desired experience for the group. For example, in group play therapy, it is very important that the leader assume a very active and involved role in the activities so as to establish the necessary role model for the group, while helping to give the clients permission to "loosen up." However, when facilitating a group fantasy trip to music, it is advisable for the leader to resume a less involved, observer type of role. The reasons for this less involved role center around (1) the group's need for therapeutic safety, and (2) observations for potential therapeutic interventions. In a fantasy trip it is common for the clients to keep their eyes closed while lying in a relaxed body position. Fantasy trips, like many other types of structured activities, often possess the potential to have a great emotional impact upon the client. As is particularly true in the inpatient institutional setting, one cannot always predict the manner in which the client will behave should he become emotionally upset. The potential is always there for behaviors that could be destructive to self or to others. Yet, by assuming a less involved, observer type of role, the leader seems to reassure the clients nonverbally that it is okay for them to close their eyes and relax and that he will perform any interventions that are necessary to maintain safety within the group.

In addition to providing reassurance of therapeutic safety, the less involved, observer role allows the leader to observe the clients for changes in affect or variation in body positions. The leader might observe changes in respiratory rate, changes in facial expressions, or areas of tension in the clients' bodies. Having made these observations will later assist in facilitating both the group and the individual's personal work by giving the leader some behaviors to point out to the client, while providing the leader with an added measure of knowledge about the client.

In general, the best guideline a leader can follow in determining his level of participation in the activity is to make himself aware of what the group might need to experience the activity to its fullest potential and what obstacles may prevent the group from having the desired experience. Having knowledge of these factors should then help the leader select an appropriate role for himself in the activity.

The next four guidelines all refer to various techniques the leader may use to help facilitate the group via the music activity. Guideline five, although seemingly self-explanatory and logical, often becomes a pitfall for many new, inexperienced leaders. If a group does not initially respond to a music activity in the manner in which the leader had hoped, very often inexperienced leaders panic and will attempt to push a group into responding to what was preplanned. However, music is a subjective experience, with no right way or wrong way to experience it or respond to it. *It is of utmost importance that the leader remember this concept!* How the leader then *responds* to the group will depend upon the leadership techniques being used. For example, in many instances, the leader may be very verbally accepting of any group or individual responses to the music activity, regardless of whether or not the new response matches his original expectations. In other cases the leader may choose to judge harshly and disagree outwardly with the group's response as a means of facilitating a desired reaction within the group. The leader might also choose to try a provocative technique, i.e. devil's advocate, in responding to the group. Regardless of which method of response is chosen, the leader must have enough flexibility in his leadership abilities to be able to facilitate where the group needs or wants to go with the activity and to integrate part of the original plan into the session as appropriate.

A clear example of this flexibility can be seen by referring back to the previous example of group storytelling. Very often a group will undertake the task of creating the story only to find themselves sidetracked into personal issues that were evoked by the music played, by the story content, or by the interactional patterns occurring in the session. The leader in such a session will quickly discover the importance of allowing time for exploration of and personal work on these issues. Allowing this time, of course, might result in the group not accomplishing the leader's predetermined task, i.e. completing the story. What the leader must be able to do, however, is flow with what the group sees as their priorities in the session. The key word, then, becomes flexibility, and flexibility begins at guideline five—a basic understanding by the leader that all responses are valid.

Guideline six is a common facilitative technique of giving feedback to an individual client, or to the entire group, about immediate behavioral observation. Within the context of a music group, this usually involves the leader verbalizing his observations about behaviors that are occurring in the activity. Very often when sharing the observations the leader can attempt to probe further with a client or group by relating the observable behavior to a stimulus.

*Example* (Therapist to group): "It seems that since I put on the faster music, not only have you been more energetic but you also seem more involved in the activity. What has been different in the group?"

In the case of a session in which the group is actively involved in music activities for the entire time alloted for the session, immediate feedback of behavior becomes even more important. In such a session the participants do not have the opportunity to process their responses to an activity. By feeding back immediate behavioral observations, the leader is able to help the participants become aware of their reactions and the stimulus in the environment. This usually encourages the participants to explore new behaviors within the session and helps them to understand their present behavior.

*Example* (Therapist to group): "There is an awful lot of laughing and smiling in the group today. Could it be that you enjoy play therapy?"

*Example* (Therapist to client): "I am aware you asserted yourself in requesting this particular song. Asserting yourself in a group is a new behavior for you."

In guideline seven, the facilitative technique involved concerns the consistent use of an activity as a resource in the session via referral by the leader to initial group or individual reactions to the activity. Very often a group, after initially participating in an activity, will wander off on verbal tangents. This may result in many issues being touched upon but none being explored or resolved. The music therapist is able to use his initial activity and the group or individual responses to it as a centering device throughout the session.

*Example* (Therapist to group): "You seem to be touching on very many important topics all at once. Maybe it would be a good idea to refocus on the initial activity and explore your reactions to it."

By referring back to initial responses to an activity, a leader can also stimulate discussion or insight on a group issue.

*Example* (Therapist to client): "Bill, you seem to have a very solid opinion about withdrawal, yet the song we listened to at the start of the session seems to express a different opinion. How do you feel about that?"

In some instances, the leader can refer back to an initial reaction as a method of helping an individual become aware of a change in affect and of his or her possible avoidance of an issue.

*Example* (Therapist to giggling client): "Gina, I noticed that during our fantasy trip you looked very sad and were crying. Now you look very contented and happy. What brought on this rapid change?"

The leader can also do this type of interaction with the entire group.

*Example* (Therapist to group): "I noticed that when we first began our activity people were very quiet and seemed distant from each other. Since completing the activity, there seems to be more eye to eye contact, more openness, and more closeness."

The above examples are only a few of the ways in which the leader can use his initial activity as a feedback device, centering tool, or facilitative resource. A creative leader can discover other techniques that are comfortable for him to apply, as well as those techniques which are effective within the group.

The final guideline focuses on the importance of integrating the participants' behaviors and insights from the group into settings outside of the group. In some instances, this may refer to a newfound musical skill, socialization skill, dance skill, or relaxation technique learned within the group setting.

*Example* (Therapist to nervous client): "In today's session, your body appeared more relaxed and you seemed to enjoy the music. Is there some way you could practice this same skill at home on a daily basis?"

*Example* (Therapist to client): "When you play the guitar and sing in the group, you look much more alive and expressive. How can you carry this expressiveness into other situations?"

*Example* (Therapist to client): "Carol, I noticed that whenever we have a sing-along you are very assertive in requesting songs. Would it be possible for you to be this assertive in situations with your husband, such as asking him to help you with the dishes?"

At other times, integration could involve helping the client find ways to use new insights for behavioral changes outside of the group.

*Example* (Therapist to client): "Now that you have discovered how you set yourself up for rejection, can you behave differently so as to minimize the chances of your being rejected?"

Overall, the process of integrating new skills and behaviors developed in group therapy is not always possible, nor is it always practical. In many cases time limitations in a session do not allow for such a process to begin. Also, the client may not yet be emotionally ready to begin trying out new skills or behaviors in settings that he may view as more threatening than the group, i.e. family, job, peer group. Whenever possible and whenever appropriate, it is important to encourage the clients to try out their newfound skills in settings in which the behavior would be helpful for them. After all, what realistically is the ultimate goal in therapy, if not to help the client lead a more fulfilling life outside of therapy sessions. Encouraging the integration of skills, behaviors, and insights from group into daily life is one large step toward this goal.

To summarize briefly the content of this chapter, there are eight basic guidelines for assisting the potential leader in planning, implementing, and facilitating a group music therapy session. When planning the session, the leader must take into consideration such factors as physical, emotional, and environmental limitations that are existent within the group, the different interests of various cultural and age groups, and the level of functioning of both the group and its individual members. The leader's role in the music activity should be dependent upon group and individual needs.

When facilitating the session, the leader must display flexibility in his role as the leader. This flexibility begins at a point at which the leader is able to realize that all interpretations and responses to an activity are valid responses, regardless of whether or not he agrees with them. The leader can then apply various feedback devices connected to the activity to help facilitate the group. It is also advisable that, whenever appropriate, the leader encourage the integration of new skills, behaviors, and insights discovered in the group into settings outside of the group.

# Chapter III

# DEVELOPMENT OF GROUP
# STAGES THROUGH MUSIC

> Maybe there's a chance
> For me to go back
> Now that I have some direction;
> It sure would be nice to be back home,
> Where there's love and affection.*

T he following chapter will focus exclusively on the use of a music
activity at the start of a session to stimulate discussion, personal
work, or group process within the group. To do this, the development of
a music therapy group has been divided into three different stages, each
of which will be discussed separately. With the explanation of each stage,
suggestions for music and music activities appropriate to that stage of
development will be provided.

In its beginning stage of development, the most critical need within
the group is to develop a feeling of cohesiveness or we-ness and a feeling
of trust among the participants. While in this stage of development,
sessions are characterized by factors such as an unwillingness to share
with or be supportive of fellow group members. The group has not yet
developed a concrete set of standards or expectations and lacks any
formal rules or limitations. This can typically result in a general feeling
of insecurity and uncertainty among the group members. Before any
further work can occur within the group, it is imperative that these
particular issues be resolved to the satisfaction of the participants. Realistically speaking, very few participants will be willing to share the work on
personal problems in a setting in which they feel little or no trust and
support. Therefore, the leader must first introduce to the group music
activities that will promote feelings of cohesiveness, trust, and security,
as well as activities that will invite sharing in a nonthreatening way.

---

*From "Home," by Charlie Smalls, as recorded by Diana Ross in *The Wiz*, © 1974, 1975, and 1978 by Fox
Fanfare Music, Inc.; all rights reserved. Used by permission.

One of the most effective methods of developing a feeling of cohesiveness or we-ness in a group is to focus on and accomplish a specified goal or task that requires the participation and cooperation of all the members. While working toward the specified goal, there are no longer eight to ten individuals doing their own thing but a group working toward an assigned task. If and when the task is accomplished, there typically develops a feeling of "we-ness," where there was previously a feeling of "I-ness."

In Chapter II, the example of group storytelling was presented as an easy, flexible, and effective method of establishing cohesiveness. However, some groups may not possess adequate verbal skills to complete the assigned task in this particular activity. Therefore, a leader must have alternative goal accomplishment activities to use with lower functioning groups. One such activity would be group songwriting. The first step in the activity involves each member of the group placing a specified amount of musical notes on a large, preassembled musical staff. When everyone in the group has added their notes, the leader plays the composition on a piano, preferably adding several appropriate chords to the piece. The remainder of the session involves the group selecting a title for their composition and then signing their names next to the staff as co-authors of the piece.

A more verbal group might also apply a similar method for songwriting with the inclusion of lyrics to the simple melody. While these are only several suggestions for activities to promote goal accomplishment, the creative leader and musician can certainly develop other goal-oriented activities that are appropriate for a particular group. One of the most important factors in this method of developing group cohesiveness is that the group feels reinforced for their efforts. The product itself, i.e. the story, the song, etc., will very often provide adequate reinforcement. Occasionally, however, the leader may supply verbal reinforcement or elicit verbal reinforcement from the clients themselves. In the long run, the leader's tone of voice and the value that he places on being a group will have a direct impact on the development of cohesiveness within the group.

Another method for promoting cohesiveness within a group is the establishment of group standards or a specified purpose for the group. This can initially be established by realizing and focusing on what the clients have in common. In group music therapy, one method of focusing on the group purpose is the establishment of a group theme song. For example, a group in which drug and alcohol abuse is a common problem for the clients may wish to select a theme song that expresses ideas against drug abuse. One such song might be "Kicks,"[13] an early 1960s antidrug song. The song can then be played however often the clients wish to hear it (usually at the start or the end of each session) as a means of emphasizing their common purpose.

In groups in which membership is open ended, it is common for new members to join the group while old members leave. With this in mind, it will also be common for group standards or purposes to change. Therefore, the group theme song may also change from time to time. However, having a group song to emphasize the common purpose of the group's members once again helps to develop that feeling of we-ness that is so important in group development.

One final method that is also effective at establishing cohesiveness in a group is to have the members focus upon a crisis or problem situation and attempt to resolve it. The extreme example of how crisis promotes cohesiveness comes when a large group of people are confronted with a common crisis and must work together to survive. For example, when a large city becomes paralyzed by a huge snowstorm, it is not uncommon to see residents of various neighborhoods working together to survive the elements. This then leads to a feeling of support and comradery or, once again, we-ness. The same concept can be developed on a smaller level to fit the group therapy setting. While the music therapist cannot create a snowstorm for his group, he can certainly play a song that describes a crisis that the group members may have in common, i.e. family crisis, suicide attempts, common physical handicap, etc. The clients are then encouraged to confront their common crisis together, in the group session, so as to emphasize working together and providing support for one another.

One example of a common crisis that might occur within a group is that of divorce. Divorce, when it occurs, is inevitably a huge crisis for the people involved, as it usually evokes overwhelming feelings of sadness, hurt, anger, abandonment, fear, frustration, and/or guilt. It is possible for a specific group to at one time be comprised of clients who are currently in the process of divorcing their mates, clients whose parents are currently in the process of obtaining a divorce, or clients who have had or are anticipating having some close involvement with a divorce situation. For whatever the reasons, divorce also seems to be a common

---

[13]"Kicks," recorded by Paul Revere and the Raiders on Columbia Records.

topic for popular songs, e.g. "With Pen in Hand,"[14] "Daddy's Little Man,"[15] "Autumn Of My Life,"[16] "There Never Was A Day,"[17] "Changes,"[18] and "You'd Better Sit Down Kids."[19] by selecting and playing one of these songs, the leader confronts the group with the subject of divorce and the feelings surrounding it and, thus, attempts to have the clients work together on exploring a common crisis.

Also common in this first stage of development is a lack of interaction, trust, or sharing among the members of the group. Very often this is the result of a fear of talking in a group of people or fear of rejection. One method of resolving this fear is to design an activity that will build interaction in steps, i.e. moving from diads, to subgroups, to full group. For example, at the start of a session, the leader might play a song for the group, then ask group members to choose a partner and discuss between them any reactions they had to the song. By starting in the diad formation, the members are being asked to trust and make contact with only one person in the group instead of seven or eight people all at once.

After the diads have had about ten minutes to share their reactions to the song, the clients are asked to join their diads to form two subgroups. A second song introducing a more intimate[20] topic is played for the group, and the clients are asked to share reactions to the song while in their subgroups. By introducing what the group might perceive as a more intimate topic, the leader is inviting more intimate verbal sharing among larger groups of people. The result of this process can be that the clients will begin to trust one another more.

The final step in the activity is for the two subgroups to come together, thus re-forming the original full group. A third song introducing another intimate topic is played for the group, and the members are asked to share their reactions or thoughts on the topic with the full group. The result of the session, then, is that clients who may have initially been a

---

[14]"Pen In Hand," recorded by Bobby Goldsboro on United Artists Records.

[15]"Daddy's Little Man," recorded by Mac Davis on Columbia Records.

[16]"Autumn of My Life," recorded by Bobby Goldsboro on United Artists Records.

[17]"Never Was A Day," recorded by The 5th Dimension on Bell Records.

[18]"Changes," recorded by Olivia Newton-John on MCA Records.

[19]"You'd Better Sit Down Kids," recorded by Sonny and Cher on Kapp Records.

[20]Throughout the book, the terms *intimate* and *intimacy* will be used. *Intimate* will be defined as something that is close and/or confidential to something, or the act of one person becoming close or closer to another person or group of people. *Intimacy* will then refer to closeness or confidentiality between people.

fearful and quiet group are now making verbal contact with each other, while trusting each other enough to share their thoughts and feelings about intimate topics.

Another method for stimulating sharing and interaction involves having each member share something about his or her personality or life in a way that is nonthreatening. In group music therapy, one activity that stimulates sharing is a game entitled I've Got A Secret. At the start of a session using this activity, each participant in the group is given a list of song titles, a small piece of paper, and a pencil. The participants are then asked to write on the piece of paper one or more song titles that express something about themselves that they have not yet shared with the group. Members are also instructed not to sign their papers or to show them to anyone else. The papers are collected and then redistributed arbitrarily among the participants. A volunteer then reads the titles from the paper he received, and the group is asked to share their reactions to the song titles, i.e. what do these titles tell you about someone, how would you feel toward someone who shared this about himself, etc. Members are invited to tell the group which song titles are theirs after the group has reacted to them, although this step is not mandatory. The result of this activity is that members are allowed to hear people's reactions to what they are sharing about themselves before they share it directly with the people. This sets up a less threatening situation and, thus, can promote further sharing in the group.

This same activity can also be done with the leader actually playing the songs that the group members chose for themselves. This, however, requires the leader to supply a large selection of records or for the participants to be notified prior to the session of the assignment so that they can bring records.

A second activity that can promote sharing something about one's life or personality is entitled Musical Rope. This activity, as will be seen, offers slightly more structure and, therefore, would be appropriate for a lower functioning group of individuals. In Musical Rope, the group members sit in a circle surrounding a rope that lines the inside of the circle. On the rope is a small ring or bead. While some background music is played, the ring or bead is passed around the rope, from one member to the next. When the music is stopped, the group member holding the ring or bead answers a predetermined question about himself. Initially the predetermined question is of a general nature, e.g. who is your favorite movie star? After the ring has gone around several times, with the music stopping periodically, and several members have answered the question, a new question is selected either by the leader or by the group. As the activity progresses, the questions become more personal so as to encourage more intimacy in the sharing process. The result of the activity is that, once again, a group of individuals is beginning to share on an intimate level, thus encouraging feelings of closeness and support.

Before continuing into the next stage of group development, it should once again be emphasized that when developing an activity to foster sharing and trust, it is important to begin at a nonthreatening level. Throughout the session a group can then work at its own pace toward increased intimacy and closeness in the sharing process.

Once the music therapy group has established a satisfactory feeling of cohesiveness and has instituted verbal sharing and supportive behaviors, it will usually move to a second stage of development referred to as insight.[21] This particular stage is characterized by participants gaining understanding of their personal issues, exploration of family-related issues, and insight into the group's dynamics and each individual's role in the dynamics. Interaction in this second stage very often focuses on problem solving and on understanding why someone behaves in a particular manner. While in this stage, the main objectives are for the participants to begin gaining awareness about themselves and the role they play in their environment as well as to begin formulating solutions to their problems.

The most common method for facilitating insight in a music therapy group is to encourage discussion on a topic applicable to the group members. One effective means of beginning this process is for the group members to listen to a song that expresses feelings and ideas about a common group topic and then discuss the song (the process is referred to as active listening). As in the example given in Chapter I with the song "Lyin' Eyes," most groups will begin discussing the issue in general terms or as it relates to a situation outside of themselves. The ultimate goal in the session, however, is for the clients to apply the problem and solutions to their own individual situations. It is important to emphasize to the members that, most of the time, there is no one specific right answer or one specific topic of insight that fits everyone. Answers and awarenesses will frequently be different for each member of the group,

---

[21]The term *insight* will be used to refer to an understanding or perception about oneself and/or those around one.

according to his or her individual situation. By sharing ideas about the topic, however, participants are very often able to discover what answers and awarenesses are most applicable to their own situations.

A second activity format for encouraging discussion on a specified topic is the use of a fantasy trip done to music. While in this second stage of development, the primary purpose of the fantasy experience is twofold. The first is to encourage interpretation of individual fantasy as it relates to a therapeutic issue. For example, if in the course of a specific fantasy trip a client imagines himself as a famous politician, then the leader, the client, or other group members may wish to offer interpretations of how this fantasy perception relates to the client's self-concept. This type of interpretation provides the client the opportunity for increased introspection and new stimulus for thought.

The second purpose of the fantasy experience while the group is in the second stage of development is to encourage exploration of new responses that could occur in old, familiar situations. For example, let us say that a particular client has established a lifetime pattern of withdrawing and pouting each time he feels angry about something. The withdrawing and pouting inevitably lead toward depression for the client, but the pattern is so well established that the client sees no alternative method of dealing with his anger. This particular client might then be encouraged to experience a fantasy of what he really wanted to do the last time he felt angry. By placing the situation in the context of fantasy, the client is invited to go beyond his normal response without necessarily having to act upon the thought. The client thus has the opportunity for exploration in a manner that is less threatening than having to behave differently. This type of creative thinking once again encourages new insights that the client can apply to his life.

As will be seen later in the chapter, fantasy trips can serve more than the purpose of facilitating insight when the group reaches its third level of development. For now, however, it is important to once again focus on the concept of structure in an activity, as there are varying degrees of structure that can be offered in a fantasy trip.

The most structured form of the fantasy trip to music would have the leader verbally guide the group through a ten to forty-five minute fantasy experience. Selected instrumental background music would be played to create a mood. One possible advantage to having the facilitator talk throughout the entire fantasy trip is that the leader's voice will help to keep the group focused on a selected setting and topic. This type of structure also allows the facilitator greater control over the experience. In some cases, however, the clients might find the leader's verbal guidance to be a nuisance as well as a source of suffocation for their creativity. This can result in the clients building resentment toward the leader, thus inhibiting future interactions and future efforts toward creative thinking.

The second most structured type of fantasy trip that can be done in group music therapy involves the leader providing the group with a specific topic for a fantasy and then playing music with lyrics that will emphasize the topic. For example, a group working on issues surrounding separation might be given the assignment to "fantasize about the memories of the people who mean the most to you in your life." Selected background music could be the song "Memories,"[22] by Mac Davis. The song provides a consistent repetition of the word *memories* and, thus, will help to keep the group focused on its task. As with the leader-guided fantasy, however, some groups will find the song lyrics a source of interference instead of a source of enhancement.

The third most structured type of fantasy trip to music would once again involve the leader in providing the group with a specific topic about which to fantasize. However, the leader could choose to play instrumental music to create a mood, as opposed to using a song with lyrics. For example, in referring to our earlier situation of a client having difficulty in expressing anger, the group might be given the assignment to "fantasize about what I wanted to do the last time I felt really angry." Appropriate background music would be the aggressive-sounding first movement of Gustav Holst's "The Planets."[23]

The least structured fantasy trip would be one in which the leader would give the group no concrete assignment for the fantasy trip. Rather, the leader would give the group a basic setting and some instrumental background music. For example, the leader may ask the group members to "imagine yourself on a large, sandy beach by the ocean doing whatever comes natural for you at the beach." Appropriate background music would include "Environments"[24] or the first movement of Claude Debussy's "La Mer."[25]

In choosing which structure to use, the leader must once again look at

---

[22]"Memories," recorded by Mac Davis on Columbia Records.

[23]"The Planets," recorded by The Los Angeles Philharmonic on London Records.

[24]"Environments," recorded by Disel on Atlantic Records.

[25]"La Mer," recorded by the Boston Symphony on Victrola Records.

the level of functioning in his group (see Chapter II). The leader must also take into consideration the goals set forth for the session, the type of music to which the group best responds, and the possible advantages and disadvantages created by the amount of structure inherent in the activity. His decision of which structure to use will, in all likelihood, be based upon all these factors.

One final example of a fantasy trip that very often fosters creative thinking and personal introspection in a group of depressed clients is called the Perfect Day fantasy. The assignment given to the group by the leader would sound something like this: "Imagine for the next few minutes that you are able to live out what for you would be a perfect day. Fantasize about who you would be with, where you might go, and what you might be doing. This is your day, so enjoy it to its fullest." Appropriate background music might include "Come Saturday Morning"[26] or an instrumental selection to which the clients could relate and relax.

After the members have each had the opportunity to share the content of their individual fantasies, open discussion could be encouraged. Discussion might focus on obstacles that prohibit people from living out their fantasy, how the members keep themselves from living out their perfect day, or methods of adapting a fantasy to meet the reality of a situation.

For example, let us imagine that a particular client's perfect day includes his involvement with a person who realistically could never be a part of the client's day, e.g. a deceased parent, child, or sibling, a famous movie star, etc. Whereas the client may never have the opportunity to live out his fantasy with the chosen person, he certainly possesses the potential to seek out relationships that could be similarly rewarding and more reality based. Exploration of how he could seek out and form such relationships encourages new insights for the client. Included at the end of the chapter are several other themes for fantasy trips and suggestions for background music.

Another means of facilitating insight in the group therapy setting is via a system of feedback. Feedback is a communication from an outside source to a person about a specific behavior and the effects and/or results of that behavior. Feedback is a way of helping oneself and another person to consider understanding and possibly changing a behavior. It is a communication to a person (or a group) that gives that person informa-

---

[26]"Come Saturday Morning," recorded by the Sandpipers on A & M Records.

tion about how he affects others. Feedback is a way of giving help to someone. It is a mechanism by which an individual can learn how his projected behavior matches his intended behavior. Within the framework of giving and receiving feedback, an individual can also learn more about his identity and self-concept and increase opportunities in which to make decisions about change.

There are some sixteen different systems or structures for giving and receiving feedback in a group setting. Feedback can be given directly, i.e. the person giving feedback communicates directly to the person receiving the feedback, or feedback can be given indirectly, i.e. the person giving feedback communicates indirectly with the person receiving feedback by talking to a source outside of the receiver. (The previously noted game I've Got A Secret is an example of indirect feedback.) Feedback systems can be structured to emphasize individual to individual contact, individual to group contact, group to individual contact, subgroup to group contact, or group to subgroup contact. In planning a session that involves giving and receiving feedback, the leader must decide whether to have direct or indirect contact and how to structure the giving and receiving process.

The most common feedback system used in group music therapy is called direct feedback through verbal fantasy. In this system the feedback is direct and can be between group and individuals, individual and groups, or individual and individual. The procedure involves the sender (person giving feedback) describing the characteristics of or behaviors of the receiver in terms of nonhuman items. In the case of the music therapy group, these items can be song titles, musical instruments, or simple rhythm instruments.

For example, a leader could bring assorted rhythm instruments to a group session. After the group has had a few minutes to experiment with the instruments to hear how each one sounds, the leader could ask each person to choose an instrument that reminds him or her of someone else in the group. Each person then has an opportunity to play the instrument in a manner that describes the person they have in mind and then explain why they chose that instrument for that person. Along these same lines, individuals can also be asked to choose song titles that describe someone in the group and explain why (see song title list at end of chapter).

*Example:* "I chose the song title "I Can't Get No Satisfaction" for you, Bob, because you are always complaining and acting very frustrated. I usually react to your complaining by becoming nervous and defensive, and so I'm hesitant to be around you sometimes."

An important aspect of feedback is that the sender includes a statement that concerns the impact on himself of his perception of the receiver. By making the impact clear to the receiver, the sender lessens the chance of the receiver feeling attacked and, hence, keeps communication open. The sender also allows the receiver the opportunity to view the impact he has on others, which could help the receiver decide upon the course of action he should take on the behavior in question. Above all else, it is very important that the leader emphasize that the purpose of feedback is to provide an individual with a learning tool rather than provide a destructive mechanism for individuals to use with each other. When used appropriately, feedback is a useful tool for providing individual and group insights in the group therapy setting, thus opening up new avenues for personal growth.

Another method for individuals to gain insight about themselves in the group setting is to structure activities that will focus on the dynamics occurring in the group. In group music therapy, such activities are usually referred to as process games, since their primary purpose is to stimulate and/or help the group explore a process or dynamic that is existent within the group. When concentrating on the group's dynamics, the individual participants are encouraged to focus upon the role that they play in the group as well as how they present themselves to the group. In theory, the manner in which a person behaves in group therapy will be an extension of how he behaves in his family structure and in relationships with others outside of the group. For example, an individual who is used to playing the role of peacemaker or rescuer[27] in his family structure will more than likely spend his time in group therapy rescuing others from uncomfortable situations. By gaining insight about his roles and behavior in the group setting, the participant is likely to explore the healthiness or unhealthiness of a given role for him. This again opens up new possibilities for personal growth for the individual.

One effective group music therapy activity used for focusing on group dynamics is the task of making a group decision. At the start of the

---

[27]The term *rescuer* refers to the individual who attempts to stop a stressful situation or occurrence from continuing, whether in a family setting, a group therapy setting, a work setting, or a social setting. Like all other roles, it becomes destructive only when the individual abuses the role to the point that it stifles his own growth process or the growth process of the system in which it is used.

session the leader can play for the group an instrumental selection of any style. The group is then asked to decide upon a one-word feeling that describes the musical selection. Given that music is a subjective experience, with members responding to it in different ways, it will be very difficult for the group to agree upon one word to describe the selection. Whether or not a decision is ever reached is of minimal importance in this type of activity. The main focus is on the process that occurs while the group is attempting to reach a decision. For example, who took a powerful role in the decision-making process, what happened when the group got near a final decision, how did each person feel about his part in the final decision? These insights can then be related to situations outside of the group, i.e. how does this role appear in everyday life, where was the role first learned, etc. Also, the interpersonal conflicts that often surface during this type of process can be dealt with at the time they are occurring. All in all, the possibilities for new insights for each member are numerous.

A second, more structured activity for focusing on group dynamics is one called song title construction. The basic format of the activity requires each member of the group to obtain something that he needs from other people in the group while staying within the given set of rules or policies. The activity begins with the group being shown a list of six song titles, each of which has four words in it. The leader asks for six volunteers to participate initially in the activity, while those remaining are assigned observer roles. Each of the six participants is arbitrarily given four cards (face up), each of which has a single word from one of the song titles written on it. The assignment is for the participants each to spell out a song title in front of them by nonverbally obtaining the needed cards from others in the group. The game can be played several times, each time with different participants and different rules. Time should be allowed between each game for the observers to share their observations and participants to process their reactions.

One set of rules that can be set for the game reads as follows: To make a song title in front of you, you may take a card from someone else's pile. If you do this, however, you must give them something from your pile. When playing by this rule, the participant is allowed to go out and get what he needs, but only by compromising with someone else. Some of the dynamics that are frequently evoked in this game include lack of assertiveness, overassertiveness, or rescuing. Discussion might center on how each person obtained what he needed to complete the task and what feelings were evoked in the process.

A second set of rules by which the game could be played reads as follows: You cannot take anything from anyone's pile, nor can you in any way ask for a card from someone. You can, however, give one or more cards to someone else. This set of rules tends to focus the group on what happens when someone does not or cannot ask for what he or she needs. Once again, the approaches used and the roles taken by each individual can be processed and related to situations outside of the group.

A responsive and creative group can also be invited to develop its own set of rules for the game. While creating these rules, the participants are inadvertently creating rules that could govern other interaction and behavior in their group, although the leader may or may not point this out to the group as his judgment dictates.

Other variations on the rules could include using more people than you have titles for or assigning each song title a set amount of points and keeping score. These variations are more competitive and, hence, will serve to raise the level of tension and stress in the group, which could provide increased motivation for the participants.

To summarize briefly stage two in group development, the main objective while in this stage is the acquisition of insight by the participants. The insight could be about group problems or individual problems. In group music therapy, the most common techniques for stimulating insight include discussion of lyrics to a popular song, discussion of the content of a fantasy trip, use of various systems of feedback, and exploration of group dynamics and individual roles in the dynamics.

In the third stage of group development, the focus in the group changes from members talking about subjects and learning new things about themselves to working through an issue or actually trying new behaviors in the group. In other words, the focus is on doing. Because of the nature of the work being done, there needs to be a high level of trust and support within the group. Hopefully, by the time individuals are ready to undertake this step in the group, this trust and support will have been developed.

One of the most commonly held views of change emphasizes that change can only occur with sufficient motivation. One big motivator for change and personal growth in an individual is stress. The level of stress in an individual, or the amount of personal discomfort evoked by a feeling or a situation, must be high enough for the individual to want to change. If the individual is not uncomfortable within himself, there is little motivation for him to change or to grow. Therefore, the leader in group therapy very often has the task of provoking or bringing to the surface the uncomfortable feeling or issue being avoided by the group or individual. Once again, because of its expressive nature, its evocative qualities, and its personal nature, music can serve as an excellent stimulus for bringing feelings to the surface.[28]

In attempting to evoke feelings about a particular issue in group music therapy, there are two primary techniques for the leader to use. The first technique involves the application of a story song in the session. In a story song, the vocalist sings a story to music, complete with characters and setting. When listening to the song, the participants in the session are asked to close their eyes and visualize the story as it is being told. Visualizing the characters, the setting, and the plot (as opposed to visualizing words on a page) usually helps to evoke feelings that the participants have connected with the issue. Once the feelings have surfaced, the leader and the group have a starting place for processing. The format for processing in this type of session can be one of any number of activities. The group may wish to focus on one individual for the remainder of the session and help that individual work through the issues that surfaced as a result of the story song. On the other hand, the group may wish to do a group exercise to help them work on the issue brought up in the song. Very often a group may write a new ending to the story as a means of solving a problem, or clients may wish to explore their identification with one of the characters in the song.

To explore an example of the use of story song, let us take a session in which the group members have visualized the story song "Whoever Finds This, I Love You."[29] This song basically describes two apparently

---

[28]In using the techniques introduced in this chapter for stimulating feelings, it seems necessary for the beginning leader to be fully aware of the potential for stressful experiences that could occur by bringing feelings to the surface with the activities. Before attempting to use these techniques to stimulate feelings in the clients, the leader must feel certain that the members can handle the stress that could potentially be evoked by confronting the feelings. For example, many psychotics are not able to work through a highly stressful issue without the risk of losing touch with reality or escaping into a psychotic episode. The leader should know ahead of time if the individual is emotionally strong enough to reintegrate himself into a normal sense of reality after confronting a highly stressful issue. Above all else, the leader should possess the ability to facilitate the feelings via facilitative techniques used for personal growth and change, i.e. Gestalt, bioenergetics, psychomotor, psychodrama, etc. Without some ability to use these skills, the leader becomes like a downhill skier without poles. The activity stimulates and begins a process within the client, with the leader having little or no means of helping to control the outcome or steady the ride.

[29]"Whoever Finds This, I Love You," recorded by Mac Davis on Columbia Records.

lonely people, an old man and a young girl in an orphanage. Through the little girl's efforts to reach out, the two meet, develop a relationship, and then separate due to the old man's death. As frequently happens with this song, one of the clients gets in touch with the sadness he has connected to a separation that occurred earlier in his life. The leader at this point may offer the client the opportunity to express and possibly begin to resolve some of the sadness connected with this issue by involving the client in a role play or a gestalt exercise. Other members of the group may function as support systems for the client or as accommodaters[30] in the role play, thus involving more clients in the experience.

At the end of the chapter, a list of story songs is given. With the titles is a list of issues for which the songs can be used, as well as references for where the songs can be found.

The second technique that is commonly used for stimulating feelings is that of the fantasy experience discussed earlier in the chapter. Whereas fantasy trips were discussed in the second level of group development as vehicles for interpretation and as stimulants for creative thinking this technique will now be discussed as a stimulant for feelings. As was previously emphasized, when a group is working at the third stage of development, the clients are primarily concerned with expressing, acting on, and/or resolving feelings.

Perhaps an example of using the fantasy trip as a stimulant for feelings will help clarify its importance. The object of the fantasy trip being used here is to help the client move through what will be called a cycle of feelings. A cycle of feelings refers to a circular process whereby an individual begins by experiencing a specific feeling, experiences one or more other feelings, and then returns to the original feeling. The cycle may take anywhere from a few seconds to a few years to occur, depending on such factors as the intensity of the feelings, the number of feelings occurring, the circumstances evoking the feelings, and the emotional makeup of the person experiencing the cycle. For our purposes here, we will explore the cycle of feelings that could possibly occur during the course of a relationship with another person and the subsequent separation from that person. If drawn in diagram form, the cycle might appear as shown in Figure 1.

---

[30]Throughout the course of the book the term *accommodate* will be used to refer to the act of helping or assisting someone in a personal growth structure by assuming a specified role and behaving or reacting in the manner called for in the structure. The person who accommodates will be referred to as the *accommodator*.

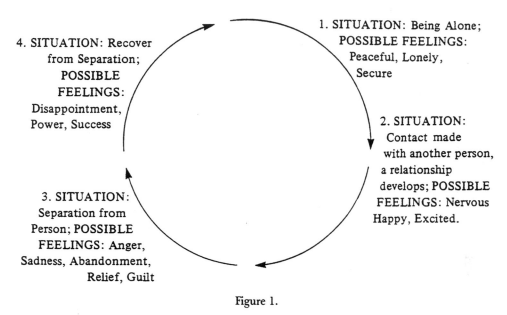

Figure 1.

As can be seen from Figure 1, each incident in the cycle has the potential to evoke any number of feelings in the individual and could be looked upon as a cycle in itself. The purpose of the fantasy trip to music is to create, via fantasy and music, each incident in the cycle for the individual, thus inviting him to experience whatever feelings arise for him at each point in the cycle. For example, each step of the cycle could be stressed through the use of three separate songs with a fantasy of "going on a journey." At the start of the activity, the participants are asked to visualize themselves inside of a place that feels safe and secure and to label that place home. In part one of the process, the participants are asked to leave their secure place and begin a journey. They can go anyplace they want on their journey, with whomever they want. This step symbolizes the first part of the cycle—making contact with someone and developing a relationship with the person. Appropriate background music could be the Sandpipers' "Come Saturday Morning" or any song about making contact, to which the group might respond or which might be supportive in helping the client become involved in the fantasy.

In part two the participants are asked to say good-bye to the friend in their fantasy and move into something new. This step symbolizes the part of the cycle labeled as separation. Possible selections for background music include "Early Mornin' Rain"[31] or "Leaving On A Jet

[31]"Early Mornin' Rain," recorded by Peter, Paul and Mary on Warner Brothers Records.

Plane"[32] by Peter, Paul and Mary. Again, any song that expresses thoughts or feelings about separation would be appropriate for this step in the fantasy.

In step three of the fantasy, the participants are asked to visualize themselves returning home or reintegrating into the feeling associated with being alone. Appropriate background music could include "Comin' Home"[33] by Johnny Mathis, "Home"[34] by Diana Ross, or an instrumental version of "There's No Place Like Home."

By the end of the activity, feelings have been evoked that are pertinent to each incident in the process, and the clients will potentially have gone through a cycle of feelings. Depending on group or individual needs, the remainder of the session may focus on one step in the cycle while touching minimally on the others. Once again, it is important that the leader have a sensitivity to both individual and group needs and facilitate the session accordingly.

Thus far, this chapter has focused on the three different stages of development existent in group music therapy while offering suggestions for activities that are appropriate for each stage. It is of utmost importance to emphasize that although the stages of development as explained in this chapter seem to follow a logical progression, in reality an actual group may be very different. For example, many groups move from the first stage of development (cohesiveness and trust) directly to the third stage of development (growth and change) while retreating back to the second stage of development (insight) at a later point in time. Very often, many of the goals set forth in the second stage of development will inadvertently be touched upon while the group is focused on its first stage of development. Also, many groups will never move beyond the first stage of development, while other groups will move rapidly through stages one and two. There are no concrete rules as to the length of time a group should spend in any certain stage of development, nor is there any concrete rule as to how a group should move from one stage of development to another. A therapeutic leader will go into a session knowing what stage of development a group is presently in and then develop a sense of when and how the group is ready to move to a new stage. For example, the leader may enter a session expecting the group to work on

---

[32]"Leaving On A Jet Plane," recorded by Peter, Paul and Mary on Warner Brothers Records.

[33]"Comin' Home," recorded by Johnny Mathis on Columbia Records.

[34]"Home," recorded by Diana Ross in *The Wiz* on MC Records.

developing insight from listening and discussing the lyrics to a song (second stage of development). In the process of listening to the song, however, several members might show signs of being emotionally upset, i.e. crying, trembling, etc. which could signal that the group is ready to work in the third stage of development. It is of utmost importance that the leader not stifle the group's development by projecting his own needs and expectations onto it. Most groups have a sense of when they are ready to move forward, and the leader must learn to trust the group's instincts. One large step toward developing this trust is for the leader to accept in his own mind where the group is in its development and realize that it is necessary and valuable for the group to be in that particular stage. By doing so, the leader provides himself with greater flexibility, thus increasing the opportunities for a successful group experience.

The following is a list of songs, story songs, and fantasy trips that can be used to evoke discussion and feelings in groups. Whereas the list does not propose to be a totally comprehensive list of all the songs that can be used in group therapy, it will hopefully give the prospective leader a starting source for applicable materials. Most of the songs could be classified as easy listening or popular tunes, although there are some variations from this classification. Once again, the prospective leader is encouraged to elaborate on the list and to choose songs that correlate with the group's interests and tastes.

| TITLE | POSSIBLE ISSUES | ARTIST | RECORD LABEL |
|---|---|---|---|
| 1. Names, Tags, Numbers, Labels | Stereotyping | Association | Warner Bros. |
| 2. I Am A Rock | Emotional Withdrawal | Simon & Garfunkel | Columbia |
| 3. Old Friends | Friendship | Simon & Garfunkel | Columbia |
| 4. Bridge Over Troubled Waters | Support | Simon & Garfunkel | Columbia |
| 5. Mr. Businessman | Materialistic Values | Ray Stevens | Barnaby |
| 6. Bus Rider | Conforming | Guess Who | RCA |
| 7. What Do I Need To Be Me | Independent identity | 5th Dimension | Bell |
| 8. Never Was A Day | Ambivalence, Divorce | 5th Dimension | Bell |
| 9. I've Gotta Be Me | Being oneself | Sammy Davis | Reprise |
| 10. The Need To Be | Being oneself | Jim Weatherly | Buddah |

| TITLE | POSSIBLE ISSUES | ARTIST | RECORD LABEL |
|---|---|---|---|
| 11. Games People Play | Deception, Games | Joe South | Capitol |
| 12. I'm Easy | Helplessness, Dependence | Keith Carradine | ABC |
| 13. Second Avenue | Aftermath of Separation | Art Garfunkel | Columbia |
| 14. Pen In Hand | Separation, Divorce | Bobby Goldsboro | United Artists |
| 15. Father & Son | Independence, parent-child relationship | Cat Stevens | A & M |
| 16. Nowhere Man | Feeling discounted, unimportant | Beatles | Capitol |
| 17. Desperado | Putting up a front, shutting people out | Eagles | Asylum |
| 18. Lyin' Eyes | Dissatisfaction with life | Eagles | Asylum |
| 19. You've Got A Friend | Friendship | Carole King | A & M |
| 20. Natural Woman | Female Identity | Carole King | A & M |
| 21. If I Could Feel | Experiencing feelings | Richard Pryor in *The Wiz* | MC |
| 22. Home | Home, feeling successful, new beginnings | Diana Ross in *The Wiz* | MC |
| 23. Love I Never Had | Anger after separation | Tavares | Capitol |
| 24. He Ain't Heavy, He's My Brother | Support | Neil Diamond | MCA |
| 25. Lean On Me | Support | Bill Withers | Columbia |
| 26. United We Stand | Togetherness | Brotherhood of Man | Dream |
| 27. All By Myself | Being alone | Eric Carmen | Flashback |
| 28. Drifter | Traveling, wanderlust | Sandpipers | A & M |
| 29. Come Saturday Morning | Traveling, making contact | Sandpipers | A & M |
| 30. Dreams of the Everyday Housewife | Feelings of being a housewife | Glenn Campbell | Capitol |
| 31. I'd Like To Get To Know You | Making contact | Spankey & Our Gang | Mercury |
| 32. Don't Cry Out Loud | Hiding emotions | Melissa Manchester | Artista |
| 33. Traces | Separation | Classic IV | United Artists |

| TITLE | POSSIBLE ISSUES | ARTIST | RECORD LABEL |
|---|---|---|---|
| 34. I Am Woman | Female independence | Helen Reddy | Capitol |
| 35. You And Me Against The World | Mother-daughter relationship | Helen Reddy | Capitol |
| 36. Changes | Lack of change, Separation | Olivia Newton-John | MCA |
| 37. Have You Never Been Mellow | Slowing down, Relaxing | Olivia Newton-John | MCA |
| 38. I Enjoy Being A Girl | Female identity | Cast: *Flower Drum Song* | Columbia |
| 39. Natural Man | Male identity | Lou Rawls | Polyder |
| 40. I Never Meant To Hurt You | Guilt feelings | Barbra Streisand | Columbia |
| 41. Tomorrow | Future goals, Optimism | Barbra Streisand | Columbia |
| 42. The Way We Were | Separation, Memories | Barbra Streisand | Columbia |
| 43. My Life | Independence | Billy Joel | Columbia |
| 44. Just The Way You Are | Acceptance | Billy Joel | Columbia |
| 45. My Way | Doing what you feel is right | Frank Sinatra | Reprise |
| 46. Don't Think Twice | Separation | Peter, Paul & Mary | Warner Bros. |
| 47. You Only Live Twice | Keep on trying | Atlantic Rhythm Section | Rolyder |
| 48. We've Only Just Begun | New Beginnings | Carpenters | A & M |
| 49. At Seventeen | Adolescent conflict | Janice Ian | Columbia |
| 50. Kicks | Escapism, drugs | Paul Revere & the Raiders | Columbia |
| 51. I Wish I Was 18 Again | Growing Old | George Burns | Mercury |
| 52. Old Folks | Appreciation of old age | Kenny Rogers | United Artists |
| 53. Old Man In Our Town | Growing old | Kenny Rogers | United Artists |
| 54. Comin Home | Disappointment | Johnny Mathis | Columbia |
| 55. All The Time | Being alone, Discovering oneself & others | Barry Manilow | Arista |

## STORY SONGS

| | | | |
|---|---|---|---|
| 1. Daddy's Little Man | Father-son relationship, Divorce | Mac Davis | Columbia |
| 2. Whoever Finds This, I Love You | Reaching out, Loneliness, Abandonment | Mac Davis | Columbia |

| TITLE | POSSIBLE ISSUES | ARTIST | RECORD LABEL |
|---|---|---|---|
| 3. Circle Game | Growing up | Joni Mitchell | Reprise |
| 4. Cat's In The Cradle | Growing up, Parental impact | Harry Chapin | Electra |
| 5. Anywhere's A Better Place To Be | Making contact, Loneliness | Harry Chapin | Electra |
| 6. Blind Man In The Bleachers | Father-son relationship, Hope | David Geddes | Big Tree |
| 7. Spring | Hope, Optimism, Life cycle | Tanya Tucker | Columbia |
| 8. Lizzy and the Rainman | Hope, Optimism | Tanya Tucker | Columbia |
| 9. That's The Way I Always Heard It Should Be | Fantasy vs. reality | Carly Simon | Electra |
| 10. Angels, Roses & Rain | Loss, Father-daughter relationship | Dicky Lee | Victor |
| 11. Summer — The First Time | Growing up, First love | Bobby Goldsboro | United Artists |
| 12. Honey | Loss, Death | Bobby Goldsboro | United Artists |
| 13. Autumn Of My Life | Loss, Life cycle | Bobby Goldsboro | United Artists |

## FANTASY TRIPS

| FANTASY | POSSIBLE ISSUES | POSSIBLE MUSIC* | RECORD LABEL |
|---|---|---|---|
| 1. Memories of People Closest | Separation | Memories (Mac Davis) | Columbia |
| 2. A Time In My Life When I Felt Content | Remembering good times | Once Upon A Time (Ferrante & Teicher) | United Artists |
| 3. Last Time I Felt Very Angry | Expressing anger | 1st Movement, "The Planets" by Holst (Los Angeles Philharmonic) | London Records |
| 4. Who I Most Want To Be | Defining changes that are desired | 4th movement, "The Planets" by Holst (Los | London Records |

*These are suggestions for background music for the proposed fantasy. The prospective leader may wish to choose other musical selections more appropriate to the group's tastes.

| TITLE | POSSIBLE ISSUES | ARTIST | RECORD LABEL |
|---|---|---|---|
| | | Angeles Philharmonic) | |
| 5. Living Out My Perfect Day | Defining happiness | 1st movement, La Mer by Debussy (Boston Symphony) | Victrola |
| 6. Going On A Journey | Open ended; no specific issues | Come Saturday Morning (Sandpipers) | A & M |
| 7. Imaginary Concert | Open ended; no specific issues | Participants imagine desired music while fantasizing a concert | |
| 8. Me In 6 Months | Future goals | What Are You Doing The Rest Of Your Life (Ferrante & Teicher) | United Artists |
| 9. At The Beach For A Day | Open ended; no specific issues | Environment (Disc 1) | Atlantic Records |
| 10. If I Could Relive My Childhood | Unfinished business, Meeting needs unmet in childhood | Once Upon A Time (Ferrante & Teicher) | United Artists |
| 11. Experiencing The Real Me | Identity | I've Gotta Be Me (Peter Nero) | Columbia |

## SONG TITLE LIST

1. Climb Ev'ry Mountain
2. The Impossible Dream
3. My Man
4. I'm Always Chasing Rainbows
5. Somewhere Over the Rainbow
6. Silver Threads Among the Gold
7. Grandfather's Clock
8. You'll Never Walk Alone
9. Yesterday, When I Was Young
10. Lean on Me
11. Ol' Man River
12. Me and My Shadow
13. Mammy
14. Somewhere
15. How to Handle a Woman
16. I Loved You Once in Silence
17. If Ever I Would Leave You
18. Bridge Over Troubled Waters
19. Both Sides Now
20. Do You Believe in Magic?
21. Gentle on My Mind
22. Hello Dolly
23. What Now My Love
24. I Want to Hold Your Hand
25. The Dangling Conversation
26. If You Go Away
27. Is That All There Is
28. It Was a Very Good Year
29. King of the Road

30. Leaving on a Jet Plane
31. Let the Sun Shine In
32. Let's Get Together
33. Light My Fire
34. My Way
35. Papa's Got a Brand New Bag
36. People
37. Raindrops Keep Fallin' on my Head
38. Can't Get No Satisfaction
39. Society's Child
40. Strangers in the Night
41. A Taste of Honey
42. Those Were the Days
43. Try to Remember
44. Turn! Turn! Turn!
45. Walk on By
46. We Shall Overcome
47. Respect
48. The Windmills of Your Mind
49. You've Lost That Lovin' Feelin'
50. Yesterday
51. The Alley Cat Song
52. Beautiful Brown Eyes
53. Beyond the Blue Horizon
54. Life is Just a Bowl of Cherries
55. Born Free
56. Call Me Irresponsible
57. Cast Your Fate to the Wind
58. I Feel Pretty
59. I'm Looking Over a Four-Leaf Clover
60. Daddy's Little Girl
61. Do You Care?
62. I Don't Want to Set the World on Fire
63. I Love How You Love Me
64. I'm A Believer
65. I'm A Lonely Little Petunia
66. Let a Smile Be Your Umbrella
67. Let's Get Away From it All
68. My Silent Love
69. No Way to Go But Up
70. Thanks for the Memory
71. Young at Heart
72. Wish Me a Rainbow
73. Games People Play
74. 19th Nervous Breakdown
75. I Am Woman
76. Thank Heaven for Little Girls
77. What Takes My Fancy
78. You Can't Ride My Little Red Wagon
79. Goin' Out of My Head
80. Whistle While You Work
81. Go 'Way From my Window
82. Blowin' in the Wind
83. Close to You
84. Hard-Hearted Hannah
85. You'll Know Me
86. Getting to Know You
87. The Pied Piper
88. We Almost Made It
89. Feeling Groovy
90. I'm Just a Girl Who Can't Say No
91. You Are My Sunshine
92. Dancing Girl
93. Hitch Your Wagon to a Star
94. Time is on My Side
95. Hey You, Get Off-a My Cloud
96. American Pie
97. Let Me Take You Higher
98. They'll Stone You
99. She's Leaving Home
100. Beautiful People
101. I Will Wait For You
102. I Wish I Knew How it Would Feel to be Free
103. The Sound of Silence
104. The Times They Are A'Changin'
105. Everything's Coming Up Roses
106. I Could Be Happy With You
107. I'm The Greatest Star
108. It's Alright With Me
109. Let's Be Buddies
110. The High and the Mighty

# Chapter IV

# MUSIC COMBINED WITH
# ADDITIONAL EXPRESSIVE MEDIA

And just maybe I can convince time
To slow up,
Giving me enough time in my life to grow up;
Time, be my friend, let me start again . . . *

In developing a music activity to meet the needs of a particular group
at a given point in time, the leader has at his disposal various other
expressive media that can be integrated into the music process at various
stages of group development. The purpose of this chapter is to explore
how four of these media, art, movement/dance, writing, and drama, can
be used in conjunction with music to help facilitate a successful group
experience.

Before exploring how various media may be integrated into the music
activity, it is necessary to look at the various factors that are involved in
incorporating the new media into the group process. The first factor to
review is why, or for what purpose, a leader would add a secondary
medium in a music group. One purpose for employing the secondary
medium is to provide additional structure to an activity. For example,
adding a specific art assignment, movement activity, written assignment,
or element of drama to a music session provides the group with an
increased amount of goal orientation and, hence, more structure. The
additional structure can very often help to keep a group focused on a
selected topic.

It seems ironic that although the addition of a secondary medium to a
music group can often add more structure to a session, the same process
can often increase the amount of flexibility the leader has to use in
evoking various dynamics within the group. The secondary medium
that is used can be applied on an individual basis within the group, or it
can be applied in diads, triads, subgroups, or as a full group task, i.e.
drawing individual pictures vs. drawing a group picture. This flexibility

---

43

increases the amount of formats that the leader may use to encourage interpersonal contact within the group, which in turn provides more possibilities for different dynamics to occur.

Another purpose for employing a secondary medium in a group music therapy session is to provide the participants with a vehicle for self-expression. A group in which the members have difficulty expressing themselves verbally might find another medium to be a less threatening vehicle for self-expression. The provision of a secondary medium may help lead the nonverbal, withdrawn members toward increased verbal self-expression, which opens up new avenues for insight and personal growth.

In addition to providing a group with a vehicle for self-expression, a secondary medium applied in a music session can also provide the group with an additional stimulus for evoking feelings. For example, the music activity may begin to evoke some feelings in the participant. With the secondary medium added to the process the participant may become even more in touch with the feeling, thus possibly increasing the chances for the client to act upon the feeling.

Still another purpose for adding a secondary medium to a music activity lies in the ability of the media to provide a vehicle for interpersonal contact. Whereas group members may not feel comfortable in initiating verbal contact with each other in the group setting, they may be able to initiate contact nonverbally via an art, movement, writing, or drama activity. The nonverbal contact can very often be more meaningful to the participants than verbal contact and can also lead to increased verbal contact among group members.

The final purpose for adding a secondary medium to the music process is that it provides an additional modality for processing within the group. For example, instead of relying completely on verbal reactions to a music activity for processing, the leader can use observations of and reactions to the drawing, the movement, the writing, or the dramatic element as a catalyst for processing the group.

In addition to understanding *why* a secondary medium would be added to a music therapy group, the second factor to take into consideration is *when* it is most advantageous to incorporate an additional medium. Typically, there are two points at which the application of a second medium can be very useful. The first is what might be referred to as a period of stagnation within the group. If and when a group enters such a period, it would be characterized by such factors as apparent boredom and understimulation on the part of the members. Discussions very often tend to be superficial and repetitive in nature, while the overall appearance of the group is that of a vehicle "spinning its wheels." The addition of a new medium into the group at this point will very often provide new stimulation for the group while giving it an extra push to break out of its rut.

The second point at which the introduction of a new medium can be effective is if and when the group members have an outward appearance of avoiding certain topics or issues. While in this period, the sessions are characterized by decreasing verbal input and interaction, constant changing of group topics by group members, oversensitivity or overreactiveness to confrontation or leadership interventions, and/or an overabundance of humor instituted by group members. Since most of the media that will be discussed in this chapter require minimal verbal behavior, their addition to the group may help break down some of the barriers against contact as well as provide the group with a concrete focus.

The third factor involved in employing a secondary medium in a music therapy group involves the selection of *which* medium to incorporate into the process. In making this decision there are two factors that must be considered. First is the level of comfort of the leader with the chosen medium. Very few leaders can successfully facilitate a group therapy session using a medium with which they feel uncomfortable. The leader's ability to model use of the medium to the group would become hampered, which could potentially cause group members to lose confidence in the leader and not experience a sense of permission to do what they are being asked. If, however, the leader should choose to employ a secondary medium with which he feels uncomfortable, it is advisable that he express his discomfort directly to the group. By being frank with his discomfort, the leader is providing the group with a model for honest behavior and interaction, which could increase the group's confidence and trust in him. By expressing his discomfort to the group, the leader may also decrease the level of anxiety the group may have attached to performing with a new medium by showing them that the object of the session is not to perfect the use of a certain medium.

Although the level of comfort of the leader with the new medium in the group is an important factor in selection of a medium, the group's anticipated level of comfort with the medium is an even more important factor. A large part of the general philosophy of employing an expressive medium in group therapy, whether it is music, art, movement, drama, writing, etc., is that the medium helps to break down resistiveness and defensiveness in the group. Yet, if the group feels extremely threatened by or uncomfortable with a certain form of expression, the resistiveness is bound to increase rather than decrease. Therefore, the leader should use caution in selecting a medium that is comfortable and effective for his group to use.

In exploring how an additional medium in a group music therapy session can be used, the leader has a choice of five basic formats from which to choose. Within the confines of each format the leader can provide the group with a highly specified, task-oriented activity or a very open-ended activity. The open-ended type of activity usually allows the group more choices of how to respond a given selection of music, whereas the more specified activity focuses more on an exact task, theme, or idea. For example, a very open-ended method of applying a secondary medium might involve the participants in expressing through the medium whatever feelings are evoked by a selection of music, i.e. draw feelings, write feelings, express feelings nonverbally, act out feelings. The more specified activity would provide the participants with an exact theme or idea to express via the secondary medium, i.e. draw your favorite childhood toy. With further explanation of the five different formats, an example of a specific activity for each of the media in that format will be given. Although the possibilities for specific activities combining music and a secondary medium may seem limitless, the introduction of several applicable activities might assist the beginning leader in formulating ideas of his own.

The five basic formats for applying a secondary medium in the music group are as follows:

1. Simultaneous application of medium and music
2. Use of music prior to the application of a secondary medium
3. Use of a secondary medium prior to the use of music
4. Use of an unspecified medium with music
5. Use of two or more additional media with music

Within the first format—simultaneous application of medium and music—the secondary medium can be used for any of the six purposes discussed earlier. The primary purpose of the music is to set a mood for or to intensify the group's experience with the secondary medium. The most common example of how music is used in this format comes from our everyday experiences with television and cinema. Feelings evoked by scenes portraying sadness, passion, joy, mystery, hostility, etc., can be intensified or further facilitated with the addition of effective background music. Although the music may often go unnoticed by the viewer, its total impact on the viewers can be powerful. In group therapy an art, movement, writing, or drama activity can also very often be assisted by the use of appropriate background music.

### Examples of Simultaneous Application of Media and Music

1. *Art:*

Assignment—Group members are asked to individually draw a picture of a favorite childhood toy.

Background Music—"Memories" by Mac Davis, or instrumental versions of various songs that are popular in childhood, e.g. "Twinkle Twinkle Little Star."

Primary Purpose of Art—Adds additional structure, provides stimulus for evoking feelings, provides vehicle for processing.

Purpose of Music—Evokes mood required to focus on aspects of childhood. Feelings of happiness, sadness, or playfulness are very often evoked by the activity. Processing might explore how adults play (or don't play) in their lives now.

2. *Movement:*

Assignment—Each participant is asked to select a partner. The partners take turns mirroring one another's facial expressions and body movements.

Background Music—Alternate music that expresses different moods and feelings.

Primary Purpose of Movement—Provides a dyad format, encourages self-expression, adds additional structure, encourages interpersonal contact, and provides a vehicle for processing.

Purpose of Music—Stimulates various feelings or ideas to be mirrored. The activity fosters body awareness as well as exploration of methods for expressing oneself. Processing might focus on the experience of each individual or on the observations of each other.

3. *Writing:*

Assignment—Each participant is asked to write down on paper one thing he or she likes about him/herself. Each person passes the paper to the left, and the person receiving the paper writes down one thing he or she likes about the person whose paper he or she has. Some background music is played; each time the music is stopped the papers are passed to the left, and the assignment is repeated until each person receives his or her own paper back.

Background Music—Any music that invites positive thinking or expresses positive feelings for someone.

Primary Purpose of the Writing—Fosters self-expression, provides stimulus for feelings, provides vehicle for interpersonal contact, and offers a vehicle for processing.

Purpose of Music—Supplies stimulus for feelings, adds structure to the process. The activity fosters higher self-esteem, group cohesiveness, interpersonal contact, and positive attitudes about oneself. Processing might involve each participant sharing and discussing each positive he received.

4. *Drama:*

Assignment—Participant acts out a funeral scene in which he or she is saying good-bye to someone he or she has lost, using group members as accommodators and support systems.

Background Music—first movement of Beethoven's *Moonlight* Sonata.

Primary Purpose of Drama—Adds structure, fosters self-expression, provides stimulus for feelings, offers vehicle for interpersonal contact, supplies vehicle for processing.

Purpose of Music—Helps to create appropriate mood, and helps to evoke feelings. *Caution:* This activity should only be done with a very high functioning group, as the activity could be very intense. The purpose of the activity is to provide the opportunity for someone to express unfinished feelings he or she might have for someone who has died. The group must be ready to explore and be able to deal with an issue that is this personal and intense.

Processing after the activity might include individual reactions to the drama, the use of clients as support systems for the participant in the drama, or how others felt in the roles they played in the drama.

The second format for employing a secondary medium in a music group involves the use of the medium after the music activity. As in the first format, the secondary medium can be used for any of the purposes that were explained earlier in the chapter. Most often in this format, the music is used as a stimulus for what will be done in the secondary medium, although this is not always the case.

**Examples of the Use of Music Prior to the Application of a Secondary Medium**

1. *Art:*

Music Activity—Group members experience the fantasy trip of "living out my perfect day" (see Chapter III).

Art Assignment—Each individual is asked to draw a picture of the most important aspect of his or her fantasy.

Purpose of Music Activity—Provides a stimulus for ideas, thoughts to be drawn.

Primary Purposes of Art—Adds structure, offers a vehicle for self-expression, supplies stimulus for feelings, offers a vehicle for processing.

The activity fosters exploration of letting oneself go and totally enjoying oneself. Processing might center around these topics.

2. *Movement:*

Music Activity—Group listens to any selection of music appropriate to their tastes and interests.

Movement Activity—A volunteer nonverbally uses his body or, with the permission of the other person, nonverbally sculpts someone else's body into a position that will express the feelings evoked in him by the music. Other members try to guess the feeling being expressed.

Purpose of Music—Provides a stimulus for feelings to be expressed.

Primary Purposes of Movement—Adds structure, gives flexibility in formats, encourages self-expression, provides a vehicle for interpersonal contact and for processing.

The activity encourages exploration of different ways in which feelings can be expressed as well as how well people are able to communicate feelings to others. Processing might encourage feedback or dialogue concerning these areas.

3. *Writing:*

Music Activity—Participants listen to the song "With Pen In Hand" or "Letters that Cross in the Mail" (see list at the end of Chapter III).

Writing Activity—Members are given pen and paper and asked to write a letter to someone from whom they are presently separated or whom they have lost via separation in the past. Participants are then asked to share their letters in the group.

Purpose of Music—The music introduces a theme and helps to evoke feelings within the participants.

Primary Purpose of Writing—Provides a structured outlet for self-expression as well as being an additional stimulus for feelings and offering a vehicle for processing in the group.

The activity fosters expression of unfinished feelings and encourages feelings of resolution from past relationships, which often interfere in the formation of new relationships.

4. *Drama:*

Music Activity—Members each experience the fantasy "what I wanted to do the last time I was angry" (see Chapter III).

Drama Activity—A volunteer acts out his fantasy in an appropriate manner, while others in group assist as accommodators. The participants then explore a method of realistically expressing the anger evoked from the situation. Once again, however, caution must be used in deciding whether or not a particular group is able to cope with an activity that is as potentially intense and stimulating as this particular activity.

Purpose of Music—Helps evoke and intensify feelings connected with the basic theme.

Primary Purpose of Drama—Provides a vehicle for self-expression, a stimulus for evoking feelings, a vehicle for interpersonal contact, and a vehicle for processing.

The activity encourages expression of anger in a safe environment while offering the participants the opportunity for feedback concerning their effectiveness at expressing anger.

The third format for combining music with a secondary medium has as its structure the exact opposite of the second format. In the third format, the secondary medium is applied first in the session, after which music or a music activity is added to the process. Once again the secondary medium can be used in the session for any of the six purposes discussed earlier in the chapter.

## Examples of the Application of a Secondary Medium Prior to Application of Music

1. *Art:*

Art Activity—Each member in the group is asked to draw a picture of his or her family tree, including on the tree whomever they consider to be significant members of the family.

Music Activity—Participants are asked to choose a song title (from a list provided, or one of their own) that they feel best describes each person in the family and then write the title next to the name on the tree.

Primary Purpose of Art—Adds structure to the activity, provides stimulus for feelings, and provides a vehicle for processing.

Purpose of Music—Provides a vehicle for identifying characteristics and giving feedback concerning family structure.

The activity fosters insight concerning one's role in the family while potentially evoking feelings about family roles, conflicts, and positive traits.

2. *Movement:*

Movement Activity—Each member of the group creates a movement and/or a facial expression that expresses a feeling. The members stand in a straight line and simultaneously perform the selected movements one after the other to create a line dance of feelings for the group.

Music Activity—Appropriate dance music is played; the group performs the dance together and then selects a name for the dance.

Primary Purpose of Movement—The movement adds structure to the activity while providing a vehicle for self-expression.

Purpose of Music—The music adds additional structure to the activity.

The activity helps to provide insight on different ways in which a feeling(s) can be nonverbally expressed. The activity also encourages group cohesiveness, as the members are working together to accomplish an assigned task.

3. *Writing:*

Writing Activity—The group is divided into two subgroups, with half the participants moving to each subgroup. The subgroups are given a topic relevant to a group issue and are asked to create eight lines for a song that would express their feelings on the issue. The group is then re-formed; the subgroups share their writings and combine them to create a song.

Music Activity—The leader adds chords and a simple tune to the lyrics, and the group sings the song together.

Primary Purpose of Writing—Provides a vehicle for self-expression and for interpersonal contact.

Purpose of Music—Adds additional structure to the group while intensifying the feelings being expressed.

The activity fosters expression of feelings as well as group cohesiveness via accomplishment of a given task.

4. *Drama:*

Drama Activity—Members are asked to recall two incidents that occurred anywhere in their lives and act out those incidents one at a time for the group. The incidents chosen should have evoked what the member experiences as opposite feelings, i.e. if one incident caused him to feel sad, the second incident chosen should have caused him to feel happy.

Music Activity—After acting out an incident for the group, the participant selects a rhythm instrument and uses it to express how he felt during the incident.

Primary Purpose of Drama—Adds structure to the activity, provides a stimulus for feelings, and offers a vehicle for processing.

Purpose of Music—Offers the client an outlet for self-expression.

The activity fosters insight about expressions of contrasting feelings. It also invites the sharing of past experiences among group members.

In the fourth format—use of an unspecified medium with music—the music and the secondary medium can be used in any order in the activity process. The basic difference in this format lies in the basic structure offered to the group by the leader. In this fourth format, the leader offers the individual members of the group the option of choosing the medium they wish to use, as opposed to providing them with a specific medium. This format tends to open up many new avenues for processing and growth in the group while allowing the group members more control in the session.

## Examples of Use of an Unspecified Medium with Music

1. Music Activity—The group listens to a selection of music appropriate to their interests and tastes.

Assignment—Choose any medium and use it to express whatever feelings were evoked by the music, e.g. draw the feelings, nonverbally express the feelings, write a short poem about the feelings, create a skit about the feelings, etc.

In this particular activity, the primary purposes of the secondary media are to provide a vehicle for self-expression, add structure to the process, and provide a stimulus for processing.

Processing in the session might include discussion on how effectively the feelings were communicated and how feelings can be effectively communicated in day to day situations.

In the fifth and final format, the leader adds increased structure to the process, simultaneously increasing the amount of stimulation in the group. This particular format involves the use of several secondary media in conjunction with music in the same session. One of the most obvious advantages to this format is that it greatly increases the possibilities for activity situations. As with the fourth format, the medium may be used in any order in the process and can serve any of the purposes discussed earlier in the chapter.

### Example of the Use of Two or More Additional Media with Music

1. Art Activity—Each member in the group is provided with a square piece of drawing paper and a variety of drawing utensils. The members are then asked to create and draw a record album cover that would be appropriate for them if they were to record an album entitled "The Parts Of My Personality."

Music Activity—On the back of the paper, write down the titles of songs (real or make-believe) that would describe "The Parts Of My Personality."

Movement Activity—After a brief discussion of the drawings, group members stand in a circle. Each participant moves around the circle and, for each different member of the group, shows a body position and facial expression that display a different part of his or her personality shown on the record album cover. When presenting this part to each person, the participant completes the sentence "This is the part of me that (*is seductive*)" or "This is the (*seductive*) part of me" (participant doing the activity fills in the blank).

Primary Purpose of Art—Provides a vehicle for self-expression and for processing.

Primary Purpose of Music—Gives identity to the parts of the personality and, hence, greater clarity to what is being expressed.

Primary Purposes of Movement—Gives a structured method for presenting one's identity to someone else while also providing a stimulus for evoking feelings connected with various parts of one's identity; also provides a vehicle for interpersonal contact among group members.

The activity fosters insight about self-identity and encourages practice in direct communication of identity and self to others.

Thus far, this chapter has focused on the various factors involved in incorporating a secondary medium into a group music therapy session. It has also focused on exploring the five different formats that can be used in creating an activity process with more than one medium. In referring back to Chapter III and the discussion on the stages of group development, an additional task for the leader is to incorporate the various formats and media into the appropriate stage. As can be seen from this chapter, the media discussed can be incorporated very effectively into an activity that fosters group cohesiveness and trust or encourages personal or group insight. Inasmuch as the media discussed in this chapter are all considered to be forms of self-expression, these media also become very adept at facilitating personal growth obtained through expression of feelings. What the leader must always remember is that regardless of the stage of development of the group or its level of functioning as a group, the addition of a secondary medium can only be successful if the timing is right and if the group feels comfortable with the medium. The addition of a second medium to the music process is a potentially effective tool when used properly and, hence, should be used appropriately and with all factors taken into consideration.

# Chapter V

# RECREATIONAL MUSIC IN GROUP THERAPY

Suddenly my world's gone
And changed its face,
But I still know where I'm going;
I have had my mind spun around
In space
And yet I've watched it growing.*

In the previous two chapters, the focus has been on developing and implementing music activities that would encourage discussion or personal work in selected group topics. In this chapter, the focus will shift to planning and implementing activities that will occupy the entire time allotted for a group session while promoting growth on important personal and interpersonal issues. The major difference between this format and the format discussed in the previous two chapters is the amount of time the group spends in participating in a structured activity. For example, in the formats discussed in Chapters III and IV, a group might spend approximately five to twenty minutes of group time involved in an activity while using the remainder of the session to process reactions to the activity. In this chapter, the activities discussed are aimed at involving the group in structure for the full amount of time allotted for the session, with little or no verbal processing involved. The activities used in these sessions promote personal growth on a variety of different issues and are often referred to as recreational music activities, inasmuch as their content is often recreational in nature.

For purposes of distinction and clarity, recreational music groups will be divided into four separate categories, each of which focuses on and defines a specific element of personal growth. As will be seen, there is a great deal of overlap between the four categories, as the elements of growth that they each promote are often interrelated. Also, many other elements of growth are often inadvertently focused upon while working on one of the four primary elements. However, the four primary elements to be discussed are issues that seem so common to the clients involved in group therapy and are of such primary importance in the overall growth process that they deserve maximum attention in any discussion related to group therapy.

The four categories of recreational music groups and their primary elements are as follows:

1. Learning and relearning of constructive socialization skills
2. Play Therapy, or learning how to experience pleasure
3. Constructive use of leisure time
4. Competitive games, or learning to cope with competition and conflict

Before explaining each of the four categories individually, there are three factors connected to the use of recreational music in group therapy that must be discussed. The first factor is the *why*. Why use recreational music in group therapy sessions? The primary reason for applying recreational music activities in group therapy lies in the constant overlapping of skills learned from one category into the other categories. If a diagram were to be drawn to display the relationship of the four elements of growth promoted in the four categories, the diagram would look like Figure 2.

As Figure 2 illustrates, each area has qualities that are unique to its area of focus. However, as will be seen more clearly as the chapter progresses, each area also contains skills and elements of growth that are interrelated with each of the other three areas. Given this relationship, and that many secondary goals[35] may also be accomplished while focusing on one of these areas, the potential effectiveness and importance of recreational music games in group therapy are astounding. This potential effectiveness is the primary reason why recreational music sessions are employed in the group therapy setting.

The second factor involved in employing recreational music in group therapy involves understanding when to employ the technique. Although there is no one specific point in a group's existence at which recreational

---

[35]Secondary goals will be defined as goals that are accomplished inadvertently as the result of efforts to accomplish another goal. For example, someone who loses weight so as to appear more physically attractive might inadvertently accomplish the goal of better physical health.

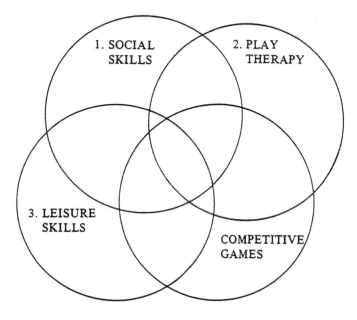

Figure 2.

music can always be said to be most effective, a brief look at the basic structure of a recreational session may give some clues to assist the leader. As was mentioned earlier, recreational music sessions involve very minimal verbal discussion while maximizing participation in a structured activity. With this factor in mind, possibly the best time to implement a recreational music session is when working with a group that is nonverbal or has difficulty discussing and integrating therapeutic concepts. Ideally the growth for the individual then occurs with minimal discussion of topics and maximum nonverbal behavior.

The second and most obvious point at which a recreational session can be maximally therapeutic is when one of the four primary elements introduced earlier is at the forefront of the group's awareness. As each of these four elements is discussed, the potential effectiveness of the recreational music session in promoting these elements will hopefully become more apparent.

The final factor involved in employing recreational music in group therapy deals with which of the four formats to use. Once again, however, there is no specific answer to this issue. Which of the four formats is used will be solely dependent upon the group's needs and abilities at the point that the session is to be held. Deciding which of the four elements of growth seems most important for the group will in all probability help the leader decide which format to employ.

Having clarified these three factors, the focus will now shift to further explanation of the four categories mentioned earlier in the chapter.

One of the problems often confronting the client experiencing mental health problems is a limited ability to use effective social skills in day-to-day life situations. This ineffectiveness might be part of a major personality disorder or it might be a temporary problem resulting from an acute psychiatric episode. Social skills problems could include ineffective assertiveness skills, limited social interaction skills, or problems with displaying affection. When present, however, problems with social skills can create added stresses to the individual who is struggling to overcome a mental health problem. Thus, the group leader may often need to address this problem as part of the treatment program.

Given that this issue of developing social skills might be a need for the group members, the leader should be prepared with activities that will assist the group in working on this problem. Ideally, the activities chosen for sessions on socialization should foster verbal interaction and appropriate physical contact in a manner that should be as nonthreatening as possible. One method of creating this feeling in the group is to apply activities that encourage group participation as opposed to focusing on the anxiety evoked in one or two individuals in the social setting. For example, structured sessions in square dancing, folk dancing, or disco dancing will foster physical contact while de-emphasizing individual participation. Touching tends to become more spontaneous and more permissible because it is part of a structured activity and is reciprocated within the course of the dance. Interactions also tend to become more spontaneous and less pressured. As is also the case with the group sing-along experience, individual anxiety connected to social encounters is de-emphasized while the fun aspect of the activity is in the forefront. By de-emphasizing individual anxieties, the leader tends to offer a more relaxed environment for social encounter and to create an air of social acceptance for each individual participant to breathe. Any music activities that help to create such an environment for the group will promote positive socialization experiences for its members, thus making it easier for socialization skills to be developed and used in othe settings.

Another problem that is sometimes experienced by the client suffering from mental health problems is an inhibited ability for play. Play can be an integral part of stress management and the ability of an individual to maintain good mental health. However, certain types of mental health problems can inhibit the individual's willingness or ability to engage in age-appropriate play activities. For example, symptomatology in the individual experiencing major depression might include low levels of energy and motivation, rigidity in physical appearance and thought process, and an inability to see or experience situations as pleasurable. To help combat these symptoms in a group setting, the leader can introduce a series of play therapy activities in session.

One of the primary causes of rigidity in thought process and body makeup in an individual is a conscious or unconscious preoccupation with what will be judged by others to be wrong or right. In play therapy the leader attempts to decrease rigidity and instill spontaneity by temporarily stifling the analytical and judgmental aspect of the personality. The leader attempts to create an atmosphere in which spontaneous behaviors are acceptable by promoting the concept that there is no right way or wrong way to play. Whatever behaviors occur while in the process of playing are acceptable as long as they are not physically harmful to self or to others.

In addition to the nonjudgmental, nonanalytical aspect of play therapy, an important element promoted in group play is feelings of increased energy and enthusiasm. With appropriate modeling by the leader, and with appropriately energetic games, the bored, nonenergetic client very often becomes enthusiastic and more motivated for self-involvement. One word of caution, however, must also be included when discussing this particular aspect of play therapy. When planning activities for a session in play therapy it is important that the leader be aware of what the group's energy level is and begin at that point. A group that appears very low in energy and very unenthusiastic will need simple, low stimulus activities to begin the session, gradually working toward more stimulating and energetic activities. By starting at the group's apparent energy level, the leader tends to make the session less threatening, thus reducing resistiveness and increasing the possibility for a successful session.

Another element of personal growth promoted in play therapy is the creation of inner sensations of fun and pleasure in the participant. Each human being possesses a part of the personality that desires pleasure and needs to have fun. Unfortunately, as we get older, work obligations, family messages, and/or social taboos often inhibit this childlike aspect of the personality. In the depressed client this side of the personality often all but disappears and is replaced by feelings of hopelessness and constant conflict. In the course of a play therapy session, the leader seeks to have the participants rediscover and re-experience this playful aspect of their personalities, if only for the brief period of time comprising the session.

When planning a play therapy session for a group, there are two basic formats from which the leader may choose. The first format, referred to as regressive play therapy, involves having the group members regress (via fantasy) to an early childhood age. While symbolically at the selected age, the group then participates in musical games and activities appropriate to that age bracket. The primary purpose of the regressive process in this format is to encourage clients to become more in touch with the playful child within them. In many instances, however, the regressive process might bring to the surface childhood issues that are yet unresolved for the client. As with other unresolved issues, the issues may be a primary source of anxiety and conflict in present situations. In this case, the issues could be a source of interference in the client's ability to play as an adult. Therefore, when leading a session in regressive play therapy, the leader must be sensitive to the possibility of childhood issues arising for the client and should allow time for personal work on unresolved issues. The resolution of childhood issues connected with playing will, in the long run, make it easier for the client to play as an adult.

The following is one example of a combined music and art activity that can be used in a regressive play therapy session. Generally any musical game that group members remember from or connect to childhood days can be used in a regressive session. Selection of which games to use in a session can be made either by the leader or the clients and can be made on the basis of a group member's movement capabilities, physical space available for the session, and the overall level of functioning and responsiveness of the group.

Activity: Fingerpainting to music.
Supplies needed: Assorted colors of fingerpaints, paper, a large table, and a record album of childhood songs.
Process: Group members are seated around the table, with the paper spread out in front of them covering the entire table. The participants close their eyes,

and the leader facilitates a fantasy that would allow the clients to regress slowly and symbolically back to the age of seven years. The fantasy process might include having the participants visualize themselves both physically and emotionally at several important ages in their lives, e.g. "picture yourself at age thirteen." The regressive process usually takes anywhere from ten to twenty minutes, depending upon the attention span of the group. Once the participants have reached the age of seven, the leader puts the selected background music on the record player and asks the participants to "play fingerpainting with your playmate." Once the group seems to have exhausted the possibilities for fingerpainting, the leader may offer several new options to the group, depending upon how much time is left in the session. The participants may wish to remain in the symbolic child stage and continue to play more games together. On the other hand, the participants may need to return to the adult stage and briefly discuss their experience of the activity. Once again, it is important that the leader display a sensitivity to the group's needs and desires so as to be able to flow with the process.

The second format of play therapy involves the participant in remaining in the adult stage while emphasizing exploration of the playful, childlike element of the adult personality. Although this format does not prescribe the use of a regressive fantasy, it is sometimes helpful to use a brief regressive fantasy as a warm-up exercise in the session.

One important rule to be followed in facilitating this type of play therapy session emphasizes the importance of timing in introducing each game. Throughout the course of a play therapy session, the group will participate in five or six different activities, each of which fosters spontaneity, energy release, and playfulness in the group members. It is important that the group not stay too long on any one particular activity. The longer a group stays focused on a specific game, the greater the chance of the group members becoming preoccupied with doing it right or of becoming bored with the game. Both the doing it right syndrome and a feeling of boredom are guaranteed methods of decreasing spontaneity in the session. Therefore, games should be changed rapidly and without extensive verbal processing.

The following examples are two of numerous activities that can be used in a play therapy session. Both activities are low energy activities and can be combined with four or five other activities to comprise a full session in play therapy.

Activity: Pease Porridge Hot Symphony.
Supplies needed: Assorted rhythm instruments.
Process: Group members together recite the first half of the children's nursery rhyme "Pease Porridge Hot."

Example: "Pease porridge hot, Pease porridge cold, Pease porridge in the pot nine days old." After saying the rhyme together as a group, each member in the group is assigned one or two of the words in the rhyme. Example: "Bob, your word is pease, Jill, your word is porridge," and so on until all the words have been assigned. The group then recites the rhyme with each participant speaking only his or her word when it occurs in the rhyme. After the group has accomplished saying the rhyme in this manner, each participant chooses a rhythm instrument to play. The rhyme is again repeated, with each person striking his or her rhythm instrument while speaking his or her word. The final step has the group performing the rhyme without speaking the words but striking their instrument at the time their word occurs in the rhyme. Thus, the group has created a "Pease Porridge Hot Symphony."

Besides creating an initial feeling of playfulness in the group, this particular activity helps to develop a feeling of cohesiveness within the group. This cohesiveness becomes increasingly important as the session progresses, since two very important elements of play are interpersonal trust and playing together.

Activity: Thumper.
Supplies needed: None.
Process: Group members are seated on the floor in the formation of a circle. Each member of the group is asked to create a nonverbal movement to represent him/herself in the game, e.g. rubbing the chin, playing a musical instrument, etc. After the group has seen each individual movement several times, the game is begun. The group members all simultaneously clap twice on their legs, after which the leader gives his movement. The group claps twice again, after which the leader does someone else's movement. The group claps twice, and the person whose movement was done by the leader shows his movement. The group again claps twice and the same person gives someone else's movement. The new person continues the game and this pattern: clap clap — movement — clap clap — movement — clap clap — movement — clap clap — movement, etc.

As the game progresses, the rhythm may be increased to create more energy in the group. Group members might also wish to add sounds to their movements so as to make the game more challenging.

In addition to encouraging spontaneity in the group, Thumper also helps to increase attention span and foster better coordination. Since the game also requires undivided concentration, group members tend to show increased involvement and contact with each other during the course of the game.

These are only two of many musical games that can be incorporated into a play therapy session. Very often a creative and responsive group will be able to invent and implement games to be played in the session. Such an accomplishment is, in many ways, evidence of the ultimate success in group play therapy. Being able to create one's own type of fun in a group therapy setting is a huge step toward creating fun for oneself outside of the group therapy setting.

Very closely related to issues focused on in play therapy activities are the issues explored in sessions devoted to learning constructive methods of using leisure time. For purposes of clarification, leisure time in this chapter will be defined as time that is available to the individual outside the job environment, school environment, and/or parenting role. This excludes time necessary for self-care activities such as sleeping, eating, personal hygiene, etc. Leisure activities are tasks that promote personal relaxation or personal fulfillment and do not carry the traditional "shoulds" that accompany work or self-care activities.

For many individuals there is a relatively equal balance in the time spent in work, self-care, and leisure activities. If drawn in a circle, this individual's life might look something like Figure 3.

However, many clients who are treated in group therapy do not allow for an equal balance in activities. Figure 4 might characterize these individuals. The results of such an imbalance occurring over a long period of time can be feelings of anger, frustration, and unfulfillment. Therefore, it is sometimes necessary for the group leader to address this issue in the course of group therapy.

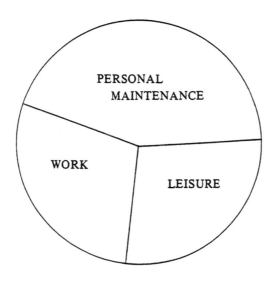

**Figure 3.**

Of course, allowing oneself an appropriate amount of leisure time is healthy only when that time is used in a constructive manner. However,

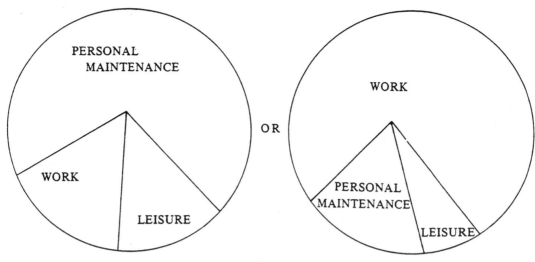

Figure 4.

some clients in group therapy may have not been able to use leisure time in constructive ways. For example, the client who abuses alcohol or drugs may spend leisure time "getting high" which then interferes with the ability to function at a job or in a parenting role. Thus the treatment process for such an individual often includes development of constructive leisure time activities.

Translating the development of constructive outlets for leisure time into the group music therapy setting could involve any number of activities. Typical formats might include group lessons on simple instruments such as guitar, piano, recorder, or autoharp. A session might also focus on music appreciation or the development of listening skills. Individual performance within the group or possibly group performance sessions are excellent formats for developing leisure skills. Group dance classes are particularly effective, especially when the participants are in an age bracket where dancing is a popular outlet for leisure time. Whatever the chosen format, the most important aspect of developing healthy leisure time skills is that the client be able to transfer the skills into situations outside of the group setting. The participant must learn how to plan for and implement healthy and constructive use of leisure time to attain the feelings of self-fulfillment sought in therapy.

The final format to be discussed for a recreational music session focuses on the use of competitive games in the group setting. The primary issue in this format is the ability of the individual to cope with competitive or conflictual situations. Whether one views it as positive or negative, competitiveness seems to be a fact of life in today's society. Competitive situations are found in business, schools, families, and leisure time activities. Interpersonal conflicts are unavoidable and must be dealt with in a constructive and healthy manner.

For example, some problems sometimes experienced by individuals in competitive or conflictual situations include physical aggressiveness, overpersonalization, complete withdrawal from the situation, or other avoidance behaviors that ultimately leave the conflict unresolved or worsened. Therefore, the group therapy session will occasionally include structures designed to help the individual become more skilled at confronting competitive or conflictual situations.

Within the group music therapy setting, competitive musical games can be used to help the participant focus on learning constructive behaviors for competitive and conflictual situations. The games may focus on individual competitiveness or on team competitiveness. It should be emphasized again, however, that if and when new, more constructive reactive behavior occurs, it should be brought to the attention of the participant and reinforced. By reinforcing the healthy, constructive behaviors in the group setting, the leader increases the possibility for those same behaviors to occur in competitive situations outside of the group.

Given here are three examples of competitive musical games. The first game focuses on individual competitiveness, and the second and third games foster teamwork and interdependence by setting up team situations. Once again, these are but two of numerous competitive musical games that can be done in the group setting. The leader is encouraged to create and implement musical games appropriate to his group's level of functioning.

Activity: Disco Nerf Ball.
Supplies needed: Disco records, a nerf ball, a stereo.
Process: Group members sit on the floor in a circle formation and are given the nerf ball. The music is started, and the ball is passed around the circle from one person to the next until the music is stopped. Once the music is stopped the person holding the ball is given a movement that he must do from that point on each time the ball comes to him. Example: he might have to pass the ball around his back before handing it to the next person each time it comes to him. The game continues, with the music being stopped periodically. Each time the music is stopped, the person holding the ball adds the required movement to his behavior before handing the ball to the next person. If a person is caught holding the ball a second time, then a second movement is added for him. Example: before passing the ball to the next person, he must

pass the ball behind his back and stand up and sit down each time the ball comes to him. As the game progresses, more movements are added, until a total of four have been added. Once someone has all four movements, he or she is out of the game if caught with the ball again. The game ends when only one person is left in the circle.

Aside from its obvious focus on individual competitiveness, the game also fosters increased energy and rapid coordination. The game can be adapted to fit virtually any group of individuals, depending on the movements or tasks used in the game.

Activity: Rhythmic Relay Races.
Supplies needed: An assortment of rhythm instruments.
Process: The group is divided into two teams, each team of equal number. Two sets of four rhythm instruments are placed on one side of the room, and the teams are lined up on the other side. A simple rhythmic pattern is shown to the group on their assigned set of rhythm instruments, e.g. hit the first instrument once, the second instrument twice, the third instrument three times, and the fourth instrument once. The race begins, and the first member of each team must run across the room and perform the pattern correctly on his team's rhythm instruments. He then runs back and tags the next person on his team, who repeats the rhythm, and so on until each member of the team has done the pattern. The first team on which all the members have completed the pattern correctly is declared the winner. The races can be continued by changing the rhythmic pattern to be played or by adding body movements to be performed while playing the rhythm instruments.

In addition to the competitive aspect of the game, the activity again fosters increased energy and interdependence within team members. The ability to function in an interdependent type of structure is very important, as once again this same type of situation is common in day to day living.

Activity: Name That Tune.
Supplies needed: A stereo, large assortment of records, and two bells, chimes, or drums.
Process: The group is divided into two teams, each of which is given one of the bells. A song is played on the stereo, and as soon as someone knows the title of the song, he or she rings the team's bell. The song is turned off, and the team whose bell was rung first has five seconds in which to name the song correctly. If that team cannot name it, the other team is allowed to hear five more seconds of the song and is then given the opportunity to correctly name the song. Each time a team names a song correctly, the team receives one point. The team that has the most points at the end of the session is declared the winning team.

Thus far, this chapter has explored four basic elements of personal growth and methods of focusing on those elements in recreational music sessions. The four basic elements discussed include learning and relearning basic socialization skills, increasing ability to play and experience pleasure, the constructive use of leisure time, and healthy functioning in competitive and conflictual situations. As might be more apparent now, the overlap of the areas as pointed out earlier in the chapter is very great. For example, games played in a session on competitive games often foster the spontaneity and energy sought in play therapy. As social situations can often bring with them elements of competition and conflict, behaviors learned in competitive game sessions overlap into the learning of socialization skills. Behaviors learned in socialization sessions are very applicable to leisure skills, as many leisure outlets involve a degree of socialization. These are but a few of the many overlaps evident in the four categories discussed. Once again, it should be emphasized that the activities presented in this chapter and the ideas discussed must be adapted to fit each individual group. These are but a foundation from which the leader is encouraged to draw in attempting to facilitate successful group music therapy sessions.

# Chapter VI

# CLOSING STATEMENTS FROM THE AUTHOR

Oh, if you're listening God,
Please don't make it hard
To know if we should believe
The things we see.
Tell us, should we run away
Should we try and stay —
Or would it be better
Just to let things be?*

With this being a revised new edition of *The Creative Use of Music in Group Therapy*, I wish to use this final chapter to briefly review the changes that have occurred in the field of mental health since the first publication of this book. In addition, I will briefly address the challenges that face the mental health practitioner and music therapist as we move into the twenty-first century.

As I look back to the first publication of this book in 1980, I am astounded by the changes that have occurred and are still occurring in the system for delivering services to those who experience mental health problems. This book was first published at a time when third-party payers and individual consumers were paying enormous amounts of money for lengthy inpatient treatment for emotional or mental health problems. At that time the large, state-operated institutions for mental health treatment were serving large numbers of clients in need of services. It seemed as though lengthy inpatient treatment for mental health problems had become an accepted practice by mental health professionals, while also becoming a profit-oriented venture for large corporations and individual practitioners.

However, the late 1980s and early 1990s brought a reversal in this trend. The increased presence of managed care groups combined with certain advancements in psychopharmacology led to a system of care that focused on short-term treatment for mental health problems while emphasizing cost effectiveness. Thus, practice in the field of mental health was now guided by concerns about cost as well as underlying theoretical principles. This has forced the practitioner to re-examine and adapt treatment methods to short-term approaches designed to stabilize the client and effect change in a cost-effective manner. This trend, while controversial to many, will likely continue into the twenty-first century.

Another trend that has emerged since the first publication of *The Creative Use of Music in Group Therapy* has been the development of specialized treatment programs and approaches for specific mental health problems. For example, it is not uncommon to find individual practitioners or programs that focus exclusively on the treatment of eating disorders. Other areas of specialization that have grown include treatment for dissociative disorders, substance specific disorders (ex-cocaine), "dual diagnosis" disorders (substance abuse combined with mental illness), sexual disorders, various types of affective disorders, and trauma associated difficulties. In addition, treatment of mental health problems of young children has become increasingly specialized in the past few decades. This trend toward specialization has brought with it significant contributions in new research and advancement of theory, while also challenging the mental health practitioner to re-examine ethical principles that underlie the practice of mental health treatment.

It is within this environment of cost effectiveness and specialization that the mental health professional and music therapist must find ways to provide qualitative intervention to the client who seeks help for mental health problems. It is also within this framework that a new generation of professionals will seek to develop careers. Such is the challenge we face in the twenty-first century and beyond.

One of the keys to meeting this challenge I believe is for the mental health practitioner to develop knowledge and skills in a variety of treatment approaches and areas of specialization. With the treatment of mental health problems becoming increasingly more complex, the mental health practitioner can best serve the client by being prepared to design intervention according to the unique needs of each client. This requires the mental health practitioner to be skilled in approaches ranging from traditional, insight-oriented treatment to cognitive therapy to behavior modification; from psychopharmacology to family systems treatment to group therapy; from intensive case management to approaches that utilize the creative arts to approaches based upon dietary intervention. For it is through this ability to creatively design treatment to meet the unique needs of the client that the practitioner can provide the best possible intervention to those who seek help for mental health problems. It is also through the development of knowledge and skill in a variety of approaches that the practitioner can best develop a career in the ever-changing world of mental health treatment.

As we move into the twenty-first century, I look forward to new developments in the field of music therapy and in the field of mental health treatment. In a world that is ever changing, the compassion, the dedication, and the commitment of the mental health professional will provide a foundation upon which to build a system of care for the individual who suffers from mental health problems.

> Living here in this brand-new world
> Might be a fantasy;
>
> But it taught me to love,
> So it's real, real, real to me . . .
> And I've learned that we must look
> Inside our hearts to find . . .
> A world full of love
> Like yours, like mine, like home!!!!*

# INDEX